STORIES BEHIND THE I

C000318854

This book was written by the First World War Study Group within the Northampton University of the Third Age [U3A]. Members contributing were:

Anne Garraway   Project Leader, Editor and Researcher
Dave Humphreys   Group Leader and Photographs
Roger Story   Newspapers and Regimental Histories
Geoff Grainger   Czechoslovakian and German Burials
Ralph Davies   Illustrations
Peter Cooch, Shena Humphreys,   }
Jan Mark, Frank Mellon and Maggie Petch }   Researchers

THE UNIVERSITY OF THE THIRD AGE

This book was funded by a loan from the Northampton University of the Third Age which is a learning co-operative of older people which enables members to share many educational, creative and leisure activities. Website: http://u3asites.org.uk/northampton

Printed and bound by Merland Copy Shop Limited, Northampton

Acknowledgements

The group is grateful to:

Alicia, Ann, Hannah, Jim, Josephine, Judith, Julia, Liz, Margaret, Pam, Peggy and Steve who gave up their time to proof read and comment on the contents.

Jon-Paul Carr, Northamptonshire Studies Manager, who gave us access to valuable source material and allowed us to reproduce it.

Alison Butler who shared her research on the Australians (see Sources).

Mike and Ray who gave their support in the early stages of the project.

Copyright

Published by
Chase Park Publishing
ISBN 978-0-9928928-0-7

CONTENTS

Page

Illustration by Ralph Davies

INTRODUCTION

The project was undertaken by a group within the Northampton University of the Third Age [U3A] which studies the First World War in all its aspects. We were looking for a way to commemorate the 100th Anniversary, on 4th August 2014, of Britain's declaration of war with Germany.

The decision was made to research the war graves in Towcester Road Cemetery, Northampton and produce a biography for each of the men and women buried there. There are 17 graves relating to the Second World War 1939-45 in the war graves section of the cemetery. Out of respect these were included in the research. In addition there are eight war graves outside the section and again these have been included.

During the Second World War several countries within Europe also fought with the Allies. There is one member of the Polish forces in the War Graves Section and three members of the Czechoslovakian Army in the Jewish Section of the cemetery. Details of the Czechoslovakian forces are on page 215 and the member of the Polish Army is on page 99.

During the First World War, there were several camps in Northamptonshire for German internees and prisoners of war. Ten Germans who died in these camps were buried in Towcester Road, but were subsequently re-interred at the German War Cemetery, Cannock Chase. Their details are on page 217.

The Commonwealth War Graves Commission [CWGC] site lists 133 people as being buried at Towcester Road. By looking at the individual graves, and checking against the CWGC, we have determined that there are 138 people commemorated in the Cemetery. The CWGC site does not list people who died after August 1921, and five of the graves at Towcester Road are for people who died after that date. These individuals are included in the research.

The members of the group feel that the stories of these people bring the reality of the war very much alive. There are a father and son buried in the same section; families where more than one son died and are buried miles apart; children who have lost both parents; mothers who lost their husbands and then their sons, and a tragic romance. The youngest is 17 and the oldest is 58.

There are also records of great achievements with two soldiers receiving the Military Medal; one also receiving the Military Cross; another one the Distinguished Conduct Medal.

There are men from far flung parts of the Empire, such as Australia and Canada, who came to our small island never to go home. To remember the Australians in particular, a service is held annually in the cemetery on the nearest Sunday to ANZAC Day in April.

As a group we are proud to tell the story of their lives.

Courtesy of Dave Humphreys

From left to right: Geoff, Roger, Ralph, Anne, Peter, Jan, Frank, Maggie, Dave and Shena

HISTORY OF TOWCESTER ROAD CEMETERY

The history begins with the decision to use Duston Hospital and Northampton General as war hospitals to which men wounded at the front during the First World War would be transferred. Men would arrive by train and be transferred to whichever hospital was suitable. As many as 188 ambulance trains arrived in Northampton over a five year period. The first train arrived on 7th November 1914. By the time the last train arrived in 1919, 9,521 cot cases (men not well enough to walk) and 13,037 sitting cases had been conveyed to Northampton. Most were treated at Duston Hospital but many went to Northampton General.

If a British soldier died in the United Kingdom his next of kin could ask for his body to be transferred to his home for burial or request that the burial take place where he died. Each soldier who died in Northampton, and was to be transferred to his home, was given a full military funeral cortège on its way to the Castle Station, now Northampton Station. An accompanying band played the Dead March, from Handel's Saul. People would stop to show their respect on each occasion.

It was decided by Northampton Borough that a special section should be set aside in Towcester Road Cemetery for military burials. The first funeral was in late April 1915 for George Ashton, who had died of wounds in Northampton Hospital (biography included on page 13).

The Independent reported his funeral, as it did all the others, and stated:

"This 'Heroes Corner' will in days to come remain to Northampton a grim souvenir of the Great War which is robbing so many homes of those nearest and dearest to them."

Burials continued until 7th December 1922. The site was extended to take the casualties from the Second World War, with the first burial taking place in April 1940 and the last in November 1947.

Earl Spencer visiting the site in 1919

John ABBOTT
(known as Jack)

Nationality:	British
Rank:	Private
Service No:	46408
Regiment:	Royal Defence Corps
Unit:	13th Battalion
Transferred to:	Labour Corps Service No. 392781
Age at Death:	26
Date of Death:	6th December 1918
Place of Death:	Sheppey Registration District
Parents:	Charles and Jane Abbott (nee Smith)
Wife:	Emily Abbott (nee Jubb)
Address:	14 Bath Street, Northampton
Grave Ref:	462.1.17950

Additional Information:

John is shown on the Commonwealth War Graves Commission as Jack but his birth was registered as John, he married as John and his attestation papers gave his name as John. The 1911 Census showed John was living with his parents, Charles and Jane, at 5 Cooper Street, Northampton. His father was a boot finisher and all the children of working age were also working in the shoe trade. Charles was born in Wellingborough and his wife and children were all born in Northampton.

Prior to being called up on the 10th January 1917, John had served with the 4th Battalion Northamptonshire Territorial Force. He was posted as Private No.13511 to the 28th Training Battalion at Maidstone. On 10th July he was transferred to the Royal Defence Corps and sent to the 13th Battalion Royal Defence Corps on 14th August 1917. The 13th Battalion had replaced the 2nd Garrison Battalion of the Northamptonshire Regiment. He was finally posted to the Labour Corps as Private 392781 in October 1917.

He married Emily on 25th December 1916 and they had no children. John died of pneumonia and did not serve overseas.

5

Family:

John's siblings were Louise, William, Eliza, Emma, Charles, Thomas, Annie, Frank and Frederick.

William served with the Royal Fusiliers as Private No. 66545 before transferring to the Labour Corps as Private No. 379327. He served in France from 28th September 1917 to 2nd March 1918 and was awarded the Victory and British Medals. He was awarded a preliminary pension of 5s 6d (£0.27½) for a period of 26 weeks on discharge.

Charles and Thomas were of an age to serve but no records can be found.

Cot case arriving at Castle Station, Northampton

Benjamin ADAMS

Nationality:	British
Rank:	Private
Service No:	F/322
Regiment:	Middlesex
Unit:	17th Battalion
Age at Death:	25
Date of Death:	23rd August 1916
Place of Death:	Northampton
Parents:	John and Mary Adams (nee Hanson)
Grave Ref:	448.3.17404
Medals/Awards:	1915 Star, Victory and British

Additional Information:

Benjamin was first mentioned on the 1891 Census living with his father John aged 71 and his mother Mary aged 50. This seems to be the second family for his father who, on the 1881 Census, was living in Newington, aged 61, a widower and working as a milliner. By the 1901 Census John was again a widower and living with Benjamin and his siblings at 120 Camberwell Grove, Lambeth. John gave his occupation as a retired tea merchant. By the 1911 Census Benjamin had left home and was working as a draper's assistant and boarding at 292 Camberwell New Road, Camberwell, London.

The 17th Service Battalion of the Middlesex Regiment was a Kitchener Battalion raised in London and was also called the 1st Football Battalion, hence the F prefix to his service number. This Battalion went to France on the 18th November 1915 and Benjamin went with them. The Battalion was part of the 6th Brigade, 2nd Division from the 8th December 1915. It fought in the Battle of the Somme, at Delville Wood in July 1916.

Benjamin died in Northampton of wounds to the right arm and a fractured thigh. His relatives visited him in hospital, according to the newspaper report of his funeral, and "expressed their very warm appreciation of the skilful attention and great kindness the deceased received from the hospital staff".

7

Family:

Benjamin's siblings were Elizabeth, Caroline, Beatrice, Amelia and his older brother, John N Adams who attended his funeral.

The 17th Battalion was the
Regiment in which Second Lieutenant Walter Tull served

James William ALEXANDER

Nationality: British
Rank: Private
Service No: 26051
Regiment: Northamptonshire
Unit: 2nd Garrison Battalion
Age at Death: 38 (Death Registration age is 39)
Date of Death: 20th November 1918
Place of Death: Northampton
Wife: Ellen Alexander (nee Cuddy)
Address: 9 Alfred Road, Paddington
Grave Ref: 446.2.17311

Additional Information:

The 1911 Census showed James married to Ellen (Ellie on marriage and Census), working as a porter in a drapers shop and born in Norwich, Norfolk. At that time James and Ellen were living at 45 Kilburn High Road, London and had been married for three years. Ellen was shown as being born in Athlone, Ireland. The only birth record found for James was in Norwich where there was a baptism on 17th December 1880 at St. Faith's Church. His mother was listed as Alice Alexandra.

The 2nd Garrison Battalion of the Northamptonshire Regiment was a Home Service Battalion. It was formed in June 1916 at Sheerness and became the 13th Battalion of the Royal Defence Force in August 1917.

Family:

James had two children who were William James (born 1910) and John Francis (1911).

John Thomas AMOS

Nationality:	British
Rank:	Trooper
Service No:	7917203
Regiment:	Royal Tank Regiment
Unit:	47th Royal Armoured Corps
Age at Death:	30
Date of Death:	22nd March 1941
Place of Death:	Warminster Registration District
Parents:	Thomas and Minnie Maria Amos (nee Collins)
Wife:	Miriam Amos (nee Tompkins)
Grave Ref:	462.17918

Additional Information:

The 1911 Census showed John living with his parents at 28 Oxford Street, Far Cotton and that he had been born in Hardingstone. His father worked as a furnace labourer.

John married Miriam in 1937 in Northampton. No children can be traced.

An In Memoriam in the Chronicle & Echo of 21st March 1942 stated that he died as a result of an accident.

John's wife Miriam is mentioned on his headstone as having died on 16th October 1941 aged 29. A newspaper item reported that "Miriam passed away peacefully away at 3 Aberdeen Terrace".

Family:

John had two siblings, Ernest W (born 1912) and Albert H (1922).

Albert ASHBY

Nationality:	British
Rank:	Private
Service No:	13292
Regiment:	Northamptonshire
Unit:	Depot
Age at Death:	25
Date of Death:	20th March 1918
Place of Death:	Northampton
Parents:	Edward Albert and Caroline Ashby (nee Reynolds)
Wife:	Nellie (nee Coe)
Address:	44 Lawrence Street, Northampton
Grave Ref:	447.2.17371
Medals/Awards:	1915 Star, Victory, British, and Silver War Badge (70061)

Additional Information:

Albert was born on 23rd October 1892 in Northampton and the 1911 Census showed Albert lived with his parents and three of his siblings at 8 Clinton Road, Far Cotton, Northampton, and worked as a tanner. He probably worked at the British Chrome Tanning Company.

He was serving a 4-year apprenticeship at the tannery prior to enlisting on 1st September 1914 at the Depot in Barrack Road, Northampton. After initial training he joined the Northamptonshire 5th Pioneer Battalion at Shorncliffe near Folkestone on 11th October 1914 and was later posted to 3rd Training Battalion, then at Gillingham, on the 12th June 1915. He was there for under a month prior to being in a draft of 50 men sent on the 7th July to France to join the 1st Battalion. On 25th September, he was wounded at Vermelles, on the first day of the battle of Loos, receiving gunshot wounds to his right leg that fractured his fibula.

In the same battle on the 28th September, the 1st Battalion casualties were 10 officers and 279 other ranks. A Victoria Cross was awarded posthumously to Captain Mountray Read of the 1st Battalion for his actions in the battle.

On 9th October 1915, Albert was transferred to England on Hospital Ship [HS] Brighton and returned to the Depot. As a result of his wound he walked with a limp. He was discharged from the army with 12s 6d (£0.62½) a week pension on 19th March 1916. He spent some time at the Star & Garter Convalescent home in September 1916 and by 1918 his pension had increased to 13s 9d (£0.69) a week.

Family:

Albert married Nellie in 1916 and they had one son, Albert Reginald who was born on 5th June 1918 (after Albert's death).

Albert had five siblings, Gertrude, Edward, Walter, Fred and Elsie. There were two other siblings but the 1911 Census showed they had died.

Fred served in the 1/4th Battalion of the Northants Regiment and embarked from Southampton on 18th April 1917 to join the Battalion in Egypt. He sailed from Marseilles on the 3rd May on board the Steam Ship [SS] Transylvania. On 4th May 1917 it was torpedoed by the German submarine U63, in the Gulf of Genoa, near Savona, and 412 people lost their lives, including Fred.

Albert Reginald served in the Second World War and died in 1990 in Jersey.

Additional Source: 1st and 3rd Battalion War Diary

George ASHTON

Nationality:	British
Rank:	Private
Service No:	5799
Regiment:	King's Own (Royal Lancaster)
Unit:	1st Battalion
Age at Death:	35
Date of Death:	16th April 1915
Place of Death:	Northampton
Parents:	William and Martha Ashton (nee Higginson)
Address:	29A Peel Street, Dukinfield
Grave Ref:	449.2.17427
Medals/Awards:	1914 Star with clasp, Victory, British and King's South Africa Medal with clasps for 1901 and 1902

Additional Information:

George was born in Dukinfield, Cheshire and on the 1881 Census was living with his father William, a cotton worker, and his mother Martha. His mother died in 1887 and his father died in 1920.

George joined the King's Own Rifles on 24th September 1898. He had signed for seven years, with five in the reserves, but extended his engagement to 12 years. At Lucknow he re-engaged to complete 21 years. In February 1900 he went to South Africa with the 2nd Battalion. He returned to the UK in August 1900, probably due to sickness, but went back to South Africa in November 1900, remaining there until March 1903. He was in Pretoria and Natal in 1901 with the 2nd Battalion and spent some time with the mounted infantry.

From there he went with the Battalion to Malta for five months and then on to India in September 1903, until October 1911. He was promoted to Lance Corporal on 8th June 1903 but he lost his stripe in 1905. Throughout his army life he had a few discipline problems. He was in Calcutta in October 1905.

He returned to the UK in November 1911, going to Blackdown, Aldershot and then went to the 1st Battalion stationed at Dover. He was in Dover at the outbreak of the war and was quickly moved to France on 23rd August 1914, aboard SS Saturnia, as part of the British Expeditionary Force [BEF].

He served in France until wounded on 28th March, at Neuve Chapelle, by a gunshot to the right thigh, which fractured his pelvis. He was taken by XI Field Ambulance to Hospital. On 1st April, he was taken to 13th General Hospital at Boulogne and on the 6th transferred to Northampton Hospital where he died of blood poisoning associated with his wounds.

His was the first funeral (see photograph below) in the dedicated section of Towcester Road Cemetery. His father and his brothers, Jim and Tom, attended his funeral.

Family:

He had three siblings, James (Jim), Thomas (Tom) and Fred. Thomas was a Serjeant with the 2/9th Manchester Regiment.

George Ashton's funeral procession

John Joseph AYRES

Nationality:	British
Rank:	Leading Aircraftman
Service No:	1306197
Regiment:	Royal Air Force
Unit:	Volunteer Force
Age at Death:	25
Date of Death:	21st March 1942
Place of Death:	Wenlock Registration District
Parents:	Mrs A Ayres, Northampton (foster son)
Wife:	Rosalie Eileen Ayres (nee Dowden)
Address:	33 Burns Street, Northampton
Grave Ref:	17268

Additional Information:

It has not been possible to identify John on any Census or military documents. There is a marriage record for a Rosalie E Dowden for the March quarter 1940 in Northampton.

A Probate record has been found for 4th May 1942 in Llandudno. His executor was Cyril Roy Ayres, a master hairdresser. It gave John's address as 33 Burns Street, Northampton and that he had died at Cosford, Donington, Shropshire. RAF Cosford is near Wolverhampton.

An article in the Northampton Chronicle and Echo reported that John died at Stafford of meningitis aged 25. His wife was Rose and he had a son John. They lived at 33 Burns Street. His brothers, Bernard and Cyril gave 59 Delapre Street as their address.

Family:

There is a birth record for a John D Ayres born in Northampton in March 1941.

Edward BARKER

Nationality: British
Rank: Private
Service No: 34958
Regiment: Royal Berkshire Regiment
Unit: 6th Battalion
Age at Death: 31
Date of Death: 9th March 1922
Place of Death: Northampton
Grave Ref: 462.17288
Medals/Awards: Victory, British and Silver War Badge

Additional Information:

Edward enlisted on 11th December 1915 and served overseas with 6th Service Battalion, Royal Berkshire Regiment on the Western Front. He was discharged on 21st June 1918 owing to sickness, aged 26, and was issued with Silver War Badge No. 410580.

The Northampton Daily Chronicle reported "that he died at Berrywood Hospital, where he had been a patient of the Ministry of Pensions since 1918. No trace of any relatives could be found. He died a lonely soldier with the British Legion and the Borough War Pensions Committee attending his funeral".

Regimental Badge

George Albert BARNES

Nationality:	British
Rank:	Rifleman
Service No:	6850566
Regiment:	King's Royal Rifle Corps
Unit:	2nd Battalion Queen Victoria's Rifles
Age at Death:	33
Date of Death:	28th March 1941
Place of Death:	Northampton
Parents:	Albert and Jennie Barnes
Wife:	Ada Barnes (nee Lewis)
Grave Ref:	17271

Additional Information:

The data collection 'Soldiers who Died in the Great War' shows George was born in India and lived in Bournemouth but this cannot be verified.

An article in the Northampton Chronicle and Echo reported that, while walking along the Kettering Road during the blackout, George stepped off the footpath to overtake a group of civilians and was involved in a collision with a car approaching from behind. Although the injury was slight George later developed meningitis and died at Northampton General Hospital. It stated that he was aged 33 and his home was 18 Beverley Drive, Edgware, London.

Family:

There is a birth record of a son John, born in late 1931.

Reginald Victor BATCHELOR
(Birth and death registered as Batchlor)

Nationality:	British
Rank:	Driver
Service No:	T/142257
Regiment:	Royal Army Service Corps
Age at Death:	21
Date of Death:	23rd June 1941
Place of Death:	Wayland Registration District
Parents:	William John and Sophia Batchelor (nee Rice)
Address:	21 Thirlestone Road
Grave Ref:	17272

Additional Information:

Reginald went to Rothersthorpe Road School and later worked as a leather dresser at Stimpson Bros. Ltd. He was a keen footballer and played for the factory team in the Northampton Leather Trades Knock Out Competition. He was engaged to Freda Kidsley at the time of his death. He died as a result of an accident.

The Northampton Daily Chronicle recorded "Death on active service as a result of an accident, Driver R V Batchelor aged 21, second son of W J of 21 Thirlestone Road."

Family:

There is a birth recorded of a Reginald V Batchlor in September 1919 in Hardingstone to parents with the surnames Batchlor and Rice.

It would appear that Reginald had four siblings, Arthur, Amy, Denis and Ronald.

Arthur served as Corporal No. 7886451 in the Royal Armoured Corps and died on 22nd March 1945. He is buried in the Ancona War Cemetery, Italy. He was survived by his wife, Mary, who lived in Piddington.

Harry Arthur Esau BAVINGTON

Nationality: British
Rank: Private
Service No: 57002
Regiment: Lancashire Fusiliers
Unit: Depot Battalion
Age at Death: 21
Date of Death: 8th January 1921
Place of Death: Northampton
Parents: Harry Thomas and Grace Elizabeth Bavington (nee Bates)
Address: 6 Foundry Street, Northampton
Grave Ref: 445.2.17295
Medals/Awards: Victory, British and the Silver War Badge

Additional Information:

Harry seems to have been known as Arthur within the family. The 1901 Census showed Harry lived with his parents at 35 Manor Road, Far Cotton and his father worked in a foundry. The 1911 Census showed the family lived at 6 Foundry Street, Northampton and his father was still in the foundry.

Harry was called-up on 9th September 1916 and served overseas with the Lancashire Fusiliers. He was discharged on 17th October 1918, aged 19, no longer fit for service and given the Silver War Badge.

Family:

Harry had three younger siblings, Albert, Louie and Grace. Records show that Albert survived the war.

George Quest BAZELEY

Nationality:	British
Rank:	Private
Service No:	146030
Regiment:	6th Dragoons (Inniskilling)
Age at Death:	28 (Death Registration age 27)
Date of Death:	14th November 1918
Place of Death:	Pewsey Registration District
Parents:	William and Frances Bazeley (nee Quest)
Wife:	Edith M E Bazeley (nee Chaplin)
Address:	52 London Road, Northampton
Grave Ref:	446.3.17316

Additional Information:

The 1901 Census showed George lived with his parents, William and Frances at 32 Sheep Street, Northampton. His father's occupation was given as shopkeeper, picture framer and taxidermist. In the Independent Newspaper in January 1914 there is an advertisement for a George Bazeley who declared he was a "specialist in fish preserving".

No trace could be found of the family on the 1911 Census. George married Edith in the March quarter of 1918 in Northampton.

George died at the Hospital Ludgershall, Wiltshire, of scarlet fever.

Family:

George had three siblings, Arthur, Ethel and Louie.

No children can be found from George's marriage to Edith.

James BOOKE
(alternate spelling Book)

Nationality:	British
Rank:	Private
Service No:	16135
Regiment:	The Loyal North Lancashire
Unit:	9th Service Battalion
Age at Death:	20
Date of Death:	31st August 1916
Place of Death:	Northampton
Parents:	Edwin and Sarah Book (nee Turner)
Grave Ref:	448.2.17404
Medals/Awards:	1915 Star, British and Victory

Additional Information:

On the 1911 Census James was working as a cow boy at Carr Wall Farm, Lostock, Bolton. He enlisted in Bolton.

The 9th Service Battalion was a Kitchener Battalion that went to Romsey in May 1915; then to Aldershot in June, and on the 26th September 1915 landed in Boulogne. James was with the battalion on the crossing. He received gunshot wounds to his left foot and was transferred to Northampton Hospital where he died.

The Independent reported his funeral and stated "Private Booke has no relatives in this country, and a brother at sea. Ten of the wounded soldiers at the hospital were the only mourners".

Family:

It would seem that the newspaper report was inaccurate. James had at least 5 siblings, Edwin; Thomas; Emma; William and Emily. However, the family history is confusing with possibly three wives for James's father Edwin.

The 1901 Census showed that James, his father Edwin, his brother Edwin and sister Emily are in the Salford Union Workhouse. His father's occupation was given as "hooker dryer for velvet dyeing". A 'hooker' was a textile mill machine operator.

Edwin, his brother, emigrated to Canada in 1913 and lived to have a family of his own.

The 1911 Census showed that James's brother Thomas was a sea apprentice, aged 14, on the River Mersey. The same Thomas served as an Able Seaman through WW1 and gained the 1915 Star, British and Victory Medals. Thomas was probably the "brother at sea" mentioned in the newspaper article.

Herbert Charles Brown's headstone
This is outside the Commonwealth War Grave Section

Herbert Charles BROWN

Nationality: British
Rank: Private
Service No: 1580
Regiment: 3/1st Northamptonshire Yeomanry
Unit: "A" Squadron
Age at Death: 19
Date of Death: 19th May 1915
Place of Death: Cambridge Registration District
Parents: Oliver Thomas Brown and Emma Brown (nee Wesley)
Address: 27 Clinton Road, Far Cotton, Northampton
Grave Ref: 273.10648

Additional Information:

Herbert was born in 1896 in Paulerspury and on the 1901 Census lived with his parents at 29 Manor Road, Far Cotton. On the 1911 Census Herbert still lived with his parents and worked as an iron moulders labourer (aged 15). Herbert was probably working at Rice's Foundry in Far Cotton. His father was a cardboard box maker.

The 3/1st Northamptonshire was a training unit formed in 1915 and A Squadron were from Northampton. The data collection "Soldiers who Died in the Great War" states that Herbert served with the Household Cavalry and Cavalry of the Line. It has not been possible to verify this.

Herbert is buried outside the war grave section (see photograph on opposite page).

Family:

Herbert had seven siblings, Olive, Ivy, Annie, William, Ernest, Ada and Horace.

Joseph Cyril BULL

Nationality:	British
Rank:	Private
Service No:	11052370
Regiment:	Royal Army Ordnance Corps
Age at Death:	31
Date of Death:	16th November 1941
Place of Death:	Northampton
Parents:	Joseph Charles and Charlotte Elizabeth Bull (nee Ager)
Address:	Lower Broughton, Salford, Lancs
Grave Ref:	17273

Additional Information:

Joseph was listed as Cyril Joseph on his death registration. The 1911 Census shows that Joseph lived with his mother and four siblings plus his maternal grandmother (Annie Amelia), an uncle and aunt (Hubert Arnold and Amelia Agar) and his cousin (Hubert Latham).

He may have married in 1934 but we have been unable to verify this.

Family:

His siblings were Winifred, Beatrice, Charles and Mabel who all appear to have survived the Second World War.

A younger nephew Gilbert Harry Agar, DFM, a Flight Sergeant, Navigator, No. 1503655, died on 12th May 1944, aged 22 and was buried at Schoonselhof Cemetery. He was the navigator in a Lancaster (103 Squadron) which crashed in Holland killing the crew of seven.

Edward George BUNTON

Nationality:	British
Rank:	Lance Corporal
Service No:	G/14853
Regiment:	Middlesex
Unit:	20th Battalion
Age at Death:	42
Date of Death:	1st March 1916
Place of Death:	Northampton
Parents:	Edward Albert and Mary Ann Bunton (nee Wadden)
Wife:	Rosina Jessie Frances Bunton (nee Williams)
Address:	Canning Town, London
Grave Ref:	449.4.17429

Additional Information:

Edward was born in Cardiff in 1874. On the 1911 Census Edward was living with Rosina and four of their children at 28 Thomas Street, Limehouse, London and worked as a shipping clerk.

He enlisted on 19th July 1915 at Canning Town in the 20th Battalion, Middlesex Regiment. This Battalion was formed in Shoreditch on 18th May 1915 by the Mayor and Borough. It was moving to Aldershot at the time he joined. He was appointed unpaid Lance Corporal on 13th August 1915 and unpaid Corporal on 3rd January 1916. He does not appear to have served overseas.

It is very likely that he had transferred to the 28th Battalion, Middlesex Regiment which was based in Northamptonshire at the time of his illness. He was admitted to hospital on 29th February 1916 with a temperature of 113°. Part of his treatment consisted of whisky and milk. He died the following day.

Edward's wife, Rosina, was awarded a pension of 29s (£1.45) for herself and six of their children.

Family:

Edward had five siblings, Harriet, Emily, Annie, Cyril and Jessie.

He married Rosina on 5th October 1901 and according to the 1911 Census they had ten children, one of whom had died by the time of the census. Only three children are listed on the 1911 Census and Rosina only claims pension for six children, Annie (born 1904), Ivy (1906), Edward (1909), Thomas (1911), Constance (1913) and Sidney (June 1916).

Typical telegram which would be received at the Voluntary Aid Detachment Headquarters in Northampton informing them of the arrival of a hospital train

Harold James BURNETT

Nationality:	British
Rank:	Private
Service No:	27255
Regiment:	Somerset Light Infantry
Unit:	7th Battalion
Age at Death:	19
Date of Death:	31st December 1916
Place of Death:	Northampton
Parents:	James and Ellen Burnett (nee Coles)
Address:	Oakhampton Cottage, Wiveliscombe, Somerset
Grave Ref:	465.1.18050
Medals/Awards:	Victory and British

Additional Information:

Harold was born in 1897 in Somerset. The 1911 Census showed Harold lived with his parents in Wiveliscombe and his father worked as an agricultural labourer. Harold was a farm labourer aged 13.

He enlisted at Taunton and first served as Private No. 2017, West Somerset Yeomanry. Sometime later he transferred as Private No. 27255 in the 7th Service Battalion. This Battalion went to France on 24th July 1915 and Harold joined them in France in 1916. He was wounded in action and brought back to England, to the Duston War Hospital. His leg was amputated above the knee and it was hoped he would recover. A few weeks later he had to have another operation and he died a few hours after.

Harold's death and funeral were reported in the Taunton Courier and Western Advertiser. The article ends with "Every sympathy is felt for Mr and Mrs Burnett and family in the sad loss they have sustained, but may they be ever cherished with the thought that his was indeed a noble end." Two of his sisters attended his funeral.

Family: Harold had four siblings, Ethel May, Amelia Rose, George Leslie and Beatrice Ellen.

George BUXTON

Nationality:	British
Rank:	Private
Service No:	038294
Regiment:	Army Ordnance Corps
Unit:	104th Company (Dover)
Age at Death:	26
Date of Death:	16th April 1918
Place of Death:	Dover Registration District
Parents:	Thomas and Emily Buxton (nee Taylor)
Wife:	Eva Buxton (nee Wilkinson)
Address:	4 Foundry Street, Far Cotton, Northampton
Grave Ref:	345.1.13457

Additional Information:

The 1901 Census showed George lived at home with his parents at 69 Euston Road, Far Cotton, Northampton, aged 10. His father was a market gardener.

On 17th February 1908, at Northampton, George enlisted in the Army Service Corps giving his age as 18. It only took nine days for the army to discover this was not true and he was discharged for falsifying his age.

The 1911 Census showed George in Rochester Borstal and his occupation was given as carter (builder's mate), aged 19. He married Eva in 1914 and they had two daughters Gwendoline Irene (born 1914) and Eva (1916).

His short service attestation showed him enlisting on 29th August 1914. He stated that he had served in the Royal Field Artillery until being invalided out in 1902. He appears to have lied about his age in 1902 and he only served for eight days. In 1914 he gave his date of birth as 18th January 1892, and stated he was working as a groom. He was given Service No. 98429 in 178th Battery Royal Field Artillery at Woolwich. He was discharged unfit on 16th October 1914. There was also a record of him serving as No. 1921 Northants Yeomanry but we have been unable to verify the Yeomanry reference. No record of his subsequent re-enlistment into the Army Ordnance Corps can be found.

George was in Dover with the Army Ordnance Corps waiting for departure to France, then went absent and was arrested by a Lance Corporal Halliday. The rest of the Corps had already sailed for France leaving only a few behind.

There was an altercation, possibly fuelled by alcohol, with a fellow soldier, Private O'Keefe, who produced his army knife "to protect himself". In the ensuing melee George was stabbed in the abdomen. The injuries to his face were treated and he was taken to hospital for the abdominal wound but it was not considered serious. A few days later the full extent of the injury to his abdomen was discovered and, even though he was operated on, he died on 16th April 1918.

Private O'Keefe was charged with murder and the report of the court proceedings shows a very confused set of witness statements. Private O'Keefe had served two terms overseas, one in Gallipoli and one in Mesopotamia from where he had been sent home ill. He had been due to join his unit in France.

The jury found Private O'Keefe guilty of manslaughter and he received a sentence of three years hard labour.

Family:

George had eight siblings, Thomas, Harry, Eliza, Ada, James, Arthur, Alice and William.

The only war record that could be found for George's siblings was for James who married in October 1911 and had two children. He enlisted on 23rd August 1918 into the 4th Northamptonshire Regiment, under Second Lieutenant C S Mobbs, as Private No. 201220 and stayed as Acting Serjeant to work in the Armies of Occupation until April 1920.

Additional Source: The Dover Express and East Kent Times

Cecil Leonard CADD

Nationality:	British
Rank:	Private
Service No:	20149
Regiment:	Northamptonshire Regiment
Unit:	6th Battalion
Age at Death:	24
Date of Death:	23rd July 1916
Place of Death:	Cambridge
Parents:	Herbert Ernest and Emma Louise Cadd (nee Hadland)
Address:	31 Newington Road, Kingsthorpe, Northampton
Grave Ref:	448.2.17407
Medals/Awards:	1915 Star, Victory and British

Additional Information:

The 1901 Census showed Cecil lived with his parents at 29 High Street, Far Cotton, Northampton. His father worked as a labourer. By the 1911 Census his mother, Emma, had died (in 1905) and some of Cecil's siblings were living with their grandparents.

30

Cecil enlisted early in 1915 at Kettering in the 8th Battalion, a training Battalion of the Northamptonshire Regiment. At the end of his training he went to France on 20th October 1915 and joined the 7th Battalion, C Company on 23rd October. Cecil may well have been part of a draft of 100 men who were sent to the 7th Battalion as replacements for the over 400 men killed, wounded or missing during the battle of Loos, near Hohenzollern Redoubt.

He was invalided home via Dieppe after suffering frost bitten feet at Étaples in December 1915. From 27th February 1916 to early May he was based at the Depot in Barrack Road. He returned to France and joined the 6th Battalion on 4th May 1916. On 14th July 1916, he received gunshot wounds to his back which caused spinal injuries. The 6th Battalion were heavily involved in the capture of Trônes Wood around this date.

Cecil was returned to England on 17th July, and he died of his wounds at 1st Eastern General Hospital, Cambridge.

Family:

Cecil's siblings were Herbert, Martha, William, Eleanor, Ethel, Joseph, Violet and Maud. Two of Herbert's brothers also served but we have been unable to find their service or medal records.

Additional Source: *David Woodhall's book: The Mobbs' Own: The 7th Battalion, The Northamptonshire Regiment 1914-18*

William Calder's funeral

(see page 32)

William CALDER

Nationality:	British (emigrated to Canada)
Rank:	Private
Service No:	18785
Regiment:	Canadian Infantry
Unit:	4th Battalion
Age at Death:	34 (35 on death registration)
Date of Death:	30th June 1916
Place of Death:	Northampton
Parents:	William and Catherine Calder (nee Fraser)
Grave Ref:	448.4.7409

Additional Information:

William was born in Thurso, Scotland on 25th August 1882. He was there at the time of the 1891 Census, living with his parents. His father was a farm servant.

In 1901 he was in a large group of young men that emigrated to Canada under a scheme to bring farmers to that country. His parents and some of his siblings followed him to Canada in 1910 and they all took up residence in Humboldt, Saskatchewan.

He attested on 22nd September 1914 at Valcartier, near Quebec City. He was living in Beckenham, Saskatchewan, and worked as a labourer. The Valcartier Camp was set up in August 1914 to help with the mobilisation of the Canadian Expeditionary Force (picture on page 64). He gave his next of kin as his brother John, who was also in Canada.

William died at the Northampton War Hospital in Duston. A photograph of his funeral is on the page 31.

Family:

William had nine siblings Helen, John, Caroline, Georgina, David, Catherine Margaret, Robert and Kitty. There were possibly two half siblings, Ann and Walter.

William Argyle CAMPBELL

Nationality:	Australian
Rank:	2nd Corporal
Service No:	1007
Regiment:	Australian Engineers
Unit:	5th Company
Age at Death:	24
Date of Death:	11 November 1918
Place of Death:	Northampton
Parents:	John Lang and Jane Campbell
Address:	"Trahalda", Princess Road, Claremont, Western Australia
Grave Ref:	463.1.17958
Medals/Awards:	Victory and British

Additional Information:

William was born in Flemington, Newmarket, Victoria in April 1894. He enlisted on 10th January 1917 in Perth, Western Australia. He had previous service in the Regimental Band of the 86th Infantry for four years and six months. He had been refused 12 months previously because of ill health.

Volunteers were sought from amongst the Western Australia railway workers at the end of 1916. Sufficient volunteers were recruited almost immediately and they became the First Australian Railway Operating Company. William departed from Freemantle on 19th January 1917 and arrived at Devonport on 27th March 1917. He arrived in France on 12th May 1917.

The unit was first based at Audruicq. It moved to Peslhoek near Poperinge, and in September 1918 moved to Conchil-le Temple where it took over from the 68th Canadian Broad Gauge Railway Operating Company. It transported large quantities of supplies for the Royal Artillery Force in Boulogne and moved coal to Dunkerque. It also conveyed petrol.

William was admitted to hospital in the field on 3rd November 1918 and transferred to Duston War Hospital, with influenza, on 6th November.

He died of pneumonia on 11th November 1918. His funeral was conducted by Rev. H G Lawson.

William was assigned to the 5th Broad Gauge Railway Operation Company in France.

Family:

William had five siblings, Gavin, Royce, Donald Clyde, John Douglas and Olive May.

The Broad Gauge Railway Operation Company in France

Thomas CARROLL

Nationality:	British
Rank:	Private
Service No:	11383
Regiment:	Queen's Own (Royal West Kent Regiment)
Unit:	12th Battalion
Age at Death:	32
Date of Death:	28th March 1916
Place of Death:	Northampton
Parents:	Thomas and Elizabeth Carroll
Wife:	Nellie Carroll
Address:	28 Crewys Road, Peckham, London
Grave Ref:	449.4.17425

Additional Information:

The 1901 Census showed Thomas lived with his parents at Kirkwood Road, Camberwell, London. His father was a stage driver and both parents were born in Ireland. The 1911 Census showed Thomas was the head of the household and a tram driver. He lived with his mother at Brayard's Road, Peckham, London. He married Nellie on 12th May 1912, but they were separated by the time of his death.

Thomas's attestation papers, dated 23rd November 1915, showed him as a tram conductor. He was posted to the 11th (Lewisham) Battalion, a Kitchener Service battalion, which trained at Catford. On 5th February 1916, he was transferred to the 12th Reserve Battalion which was then based at Northampton.

Thomas died of pneumonia. His personal possessions were sent to Mrs Maggie Carey, 28 Crewys Road, Peckham, London.

Family: Thomas had two siblings Martha and Maggie.

Harry N CARTER

Nationality:	British
Rank:	Private
Service No:	549352
Regiment:	Labour Corps
Age at Death:	29
Date of Death:	23rd January 1922
Place of Death:	Hardingstone Registration District
Grave Ref:	462.17287
Medals/Awards:	Victory and British

Additional Information:

Harry is not listed on the Commonwealth War Graves Website as he died after August 1921. Information above is taken from his memorial stone in Towcester Road Cemetery.

Harry's medal card showed he was recruited as Private No. 22951, Northamptonshire Regiment and must have transferred to the Labour Corps at some point in his service.

There was a record of the birth of a Harry Norton Carter in Cosford, Suffolk in 1892 and linked to the Census in 1901 and 1911 but there is nothing to verify this was the same Harry.

Cap Badge of the Labour Corps

Arthur Alfred CHAMBERS

Nationality: British
Rank: Sergeant Wireless Operator/Air Gunner
Service No: 1578098
Regiment: Royal Air Force
Unit: Volunteer Reserve
Age at Death: 19
Date of Death: 19th April 1943
Place of Death: Cirencester Registration District
Parents: Arthur and Eleanor Chambers
Address: 14 Stevenson Street, Far Cotton
Grave Ref: 17269

Additional Information:

There was a possible birth for an Arthur in September 1923 in Poplar but we are unable to find any other information about him.

The Northampton Daily Chronicle in April 1943 stated that Arthur was a member of the Air Training Corps and worked in the butchery branch of the Northampton Co-Operative in Abington Street. He passed out of training school about October 1941 and was a wireless operator/air gunner at the time of his death.

Family:

Arthur had a brother, Roy.

Percy CHAMBERS

Nationality:	British
Rank:	Gunner
Service No:	42093
Regiment:	Royal Field Artillery
Unit:	4th "C" Reserve Brigade
Age at Death:	31
Date of Death:	29th February 1916
Place of Death:	Northampton
Parents:	James and Emma Chambers
Address:	Mill House, Westwell, Ashford, Kent
Grave Ref:	448.4.17417
Medals/Awards:	1914 Star with clasp, Victory and British

Additional Information:

Percy was born in Westwell, Kent in 1885. His birth was registered as Ernest Percy but he appears to have preferred the name Percy as that was the name he used when enlisting into The Buffs on 22nd September 1902. His service number was 6961. He transferred to the Royal Field Artillery as No. 42093 on 26th February 1906 and served with the 88th Battery from 30th December 1909. He had originally signed for three years with the colours and eight with the reserves but kept extending his service under the colours.

In 1913 he was regarded as being trustworthy, sober, reliable, clean and a good gunner.

It appears he did not leave the UK until 23rd August 1914, when he went to France. He must have served in the front line as he received the 1914 Star with clasp but his record does not give details. He returned from France on 16th December 1916 and died at Northampton General Hospital of acute hepatitis and emphysema.

On his attestation papers in 1902 he listed his father James as his next of kin. When he died in 1916 his brother Thomas was stated as next of kin.

An article in the Independent Newspaper on 6th March 1916 recorded his Military funeral. The family mourners were: his brother Mr T Chambers, of Hothfield, Kent; his sister Mrs Manquet, of Bedford. Also mentioned is a Mr T Pullen of Willesborough, Kent.

Family:

Percy was the youngest of twelve children, Henry (born 1860), Joseph (1863), Grace (1867), Alfred (1870), Harriet (1873), Thomas (1875), Emma (1877), Edward (1878), Roseanne (1881), Edith (1883) and Daisy (1884).

Thomas was undoubtedly the Mr T Chambers mentioned in the Independent Newspaper and Harriet, who married a soldier, Leigh Reginald Manquet in June 1895, was undoubtedly the Mrs Manquet of Bedford mentioned in the same article.

**Memorial Plaque sent to next of kin of those who died
in World War One**
Further details in Campaign Medals and Awards (page 221)

Robert James CHANDLER

Nationality:	British
Rank:	Corporal
Service No:	3/10344
Regiment:	Northamptonshire
Unit:	1st Battalion
Age at Death:	41
Date of Death:	20th April 1921
Place of Death:	S. Stoneham Registration District, Hampshire
Parents:	Benjamin and Sarah Chandler (nee Ross)
Wife:	Mary Josephine Chandler (nee Law)
Address:	14 Doddridge Square, Northampton
Grave Ref:	445.4.17293
Medals/Awards:	1914 Star, British, Victory and Silver War Badge 40297. He also had campaign medals from the South African War

Additional Information:

The 1881 Census showed that Robert lived with his parents in Bethnal Green where he was born. His father, Benjamin, was a general dealer. The 1891 Census showed the family living with Sarah's sister in Bethnal Green and Benjamin was then a fish salesman.

Robert served in the Boer War with the 2nd Battalion as Private No. 5229 and was invalided home, receiving the Queen's South African Medal with clasps for Cape Colony and Orange Free State. At the time of the 1901 Census Robert was living at the Barracks of the Depot of the Northamptonshire Regiment.

By the 1911 Census he was married to Josephine and lived at 68 Green Street, Northampton. He was a theatre attendant.

Robert was recalled from the National Reserve on 23rd August 1914 to the 3rd Training Battalion and then went with a draft of 400 men to France on 11th November 1914. There he joined the 1st Battalion that was heavily engaged with the Germans. By 14th November, the 1st Battalion was reduced to two officers and 300 men.

Robert was returned to the 3rd Battalion, in England, a month later where he remained until discharged sick on 28th August 1915, a year after recall. He was given a pension of 18s 9d (£0.93) a week. After his death Josephine was awarded a pension of 26s 8d (£1.33) for herself and 23s 6d (£1.17) for their three children.

Family:

At the time of the 1891 Census, Robert had a sister Flora (aged 1). He married Josephine in late 1903 and the 1911 Census showed they had two children, William (aged 5) and Leonard (2). Another son Robert J was born at the end of 1911.

Additional Source: 1st and 3rd Battalion War Diary

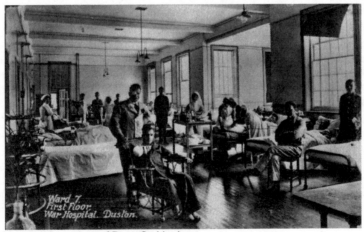

Photograph courtesy of Doug Goddard

Typical ward War Hospital, Duston

George CHAPMAN

Nationality:	British
Rank:	Gunner
Service No:	58634
Regiment:	Royal Garrison Artillery [RGA]
Unit:	113th Heavy Battalion
Age at Death:	47 (death registration)
Date of Death:	11th May 1917
Place of Death:	Northampton
Grave Ref:	448.2.17383
Medals/Awards:	Victory and British

Additional Information:

George signed up at Staines on 16th September 1915, and was posted to the Royal Garrison Artillery at Dover. He had stated that his age was 39 and had been born in Croydon. His address at that time was given as 3 Bertange Yard, Grantham, he was a labourer and gave Thomas Henry (address unknown), his brother, as next of kin. George's death registration showed his age as 47 which does not tie with his given age at attestation.

He went to France on 8th February 1916 and was posted to 113th Heavy Battery, RGA. The 113th Heavy Battery was attached to 1st Infantry Division. About a year later on 6th March 1917 he was admitted to hospital and moved to No. 1 General Hospital at Étretat from which he was invalided to England on 16th March. He was sent to Duston War Hospital where he died of chronic nephritis on 11th May 1917. Despite efforts to find his relatives none could be found.

On the 1901 Census there was a George Chapman, born in Croydon and the right age, who lived at the Municipal Lodging House, Pitlake Bridge, Croydon. and worked as a labourer.

Family:

We could find only one sibling, Thomas Henry, mentioned in his attestation papers.

Albert Lewis CLARK
(alternate spelling Clarke)

Nationality:	British
Rank:	Private
Service No:	TR10/52044
Regiment:	Middlesex Regiment
Unit:	102nd Training Reserve Battalion
Age at Death:	36
Date of Death:	4th March 1919
Place of Death:	Brixworth Registration District
Wife:	Lavinia Clark (nee Edwards)
Address:	25 Hollybush Gardens, London EC
Grave Ref:	462.1.17946
Medals/Awards:	Victory, British and Silver War Badge

Additional Information:

Albert enlisted on 8th December 1915, at Finsbury Barracks, London. He stated he had served five months in the Buffs Special Reserves in 1909. He gave his age as 33, and his occupation as shoemaker. He had married Lavinia on 22nd February 1904, at St Peter's, Bethnal Green. No children were listed on his attestation papers.

He was discharged sick on 16th October 1916 and awarded Silver War Badge No. 143971. Albert applied for a pension and stated he would return to work at Ward & Co. Ltd. when fit enough to do so. He was awarded a pension of 15s (£0.75) initially. On 16th October 1917, his case was reviewed and it was recommended that he enter a sanatorium as he was suffering from tuberculosis.

Albert was recorded as serving under the colours as a "cook's mate and ordinary military duties".

Alice Annie CLEMENTS

Nationality:	British
Rank:	Private
Service No:	W/100133
Regiment:	Auxiliary Territorial Service [ATS]
Age at Death:	34
Date of Death:	11th November 1947
Place of Death:	Northampton
Parents:	George and Elizabeth Clements (nee Blunt)
Address:	Abington, Northampton
Grave Ref:	17906

Additional Information:

The 1911 Census showed that Alice's parents, George and Elizabeth, lived with George's father at 87 Margaret Street, Northampton. They had been married for seven years. George was working as a porter and his birthplace was Stafford.

The Chronicle and Echo, on 11th November 1947, stated that Alice died after long suffering. Her mother, Elizabeth, was a widow.

Family:

Alice had two older siblings, Caroline Edith (aged 5), and George Thomas (1), at the time of the 1911 Census and two further children were born, Albert Edward (1914) and Frederick B (1918).

Albert Edward is recorded on the CWGC as having died on 21 December 1941 and was buried in the Tripoli War Cemetery. He served in the Royal Engineers Field Squadron and his number was 7883218.

George and Frederick (Fred) also served in WW2. Fred served in the Royal Electrical and Mechanical Engineers [REME]. Prior to serving in the forces Fred had worked for the railway. At some point in the war Fred was responsible for driving a munitions train, which was on fire, to a place of safety.

This is a typical recruitment poster for the Auxiliary Territorial Service [ATS] in the period 1939-45. The ATS covered many roles including driving and clerical work. The most famous member was Princess Elizabeth, now HM Queen Elizabeth II.

Arthur CODLING

Nationality:	British
Rank:	Private
Service No:	28812
Regiment:	Royal Defence Corps
Unit:	66th Company
Age at Death:	40 (Death Registration states 41)
Date of Death:	6th May 1917
Place of Death:	Northampton
Parents:	James and Elizabeth Codling
Wife:	Sarah Ann Codling (nee Wells)
Address:	53 St Andrews Street North, Bury St. Edmunds
Grave Ref:	448.4.17389

Additional Information:

Arthur was born and lived most of his life in Suffolk. His father was an agricultural labourer. Arthur married Sarah in 1898 and on the 1901 Census he was working in the gas industry, living at Eastgate Street, Bury St Edmunds. The 1911 Census showed Arthur and Sarah lived at St Andrews Street, Bury St Edmunds and he still worked in the gas industry.

He enlisted at Bury St Edmunds and first served in the Suffolk Regiment under the No. 22843. Arthur died of phthisis (tuberculosis) at Duston War Hospital and the local Voluntary Aid Detachment [VAD] arranged his funeral which started from their rooms in King Street.

His wife and children are commemorated on his headstone.

Family:

Arthur had seven siblings, William (born 1868), George (1870), Eliza Jane (1873), Elizabeth (1875), Charles (1882), Harry (1884) and Beatrice (1887).

Arthur and Sarah had two children Maud and Grace.

William Harold COLLIER

Nationality:	British
Rank:	Private
Service No:	R4/125030
Regiment:	Army Service Corps
Unit:	Remounts
Age at Death:	29
Date of Death:	22nd January 1917
Place of Death:	Northampton
Parents:	Frances Collier
Wife:	Ethel Winifred Collier (nee Elmes)
Address:	8 Kettering Road, Broughton, Kettering
Grave Ref:	448.3.17396

Additional Information:

On the 1891 Census William lived with his uncle and aunt, Joseph and Fanny Collier in Newport Pagnell. There is no trace of William on the 1901 Census but on the 1911 Census he was a boarder and worked as a house painter. In 1913 he married Ethel in Kettering.

William died at the Duston War Hospital and his funeral was conducted by the Rev. L Streatfield, vicar of Dallington. The local Royal Field Artillery provided the gun carriage.

William's wife Ethel died in 1962 aged 75 and was commemorated on his headstone.

Family:

William and Ethel had one child Horace E, born in 1914.

William COLLISHAW

Nationality:	British
Rank:	Private
Service No:	S/16145
Regiment:	Army Service Corps
Unit:	"A" Company (Aldershot)
Age at Death:	34
Date of Death:	13th June 1915
Place of Death:	Northampton
Parents:	Henry and Hannah Collishaw (nee Pacey)
Grave Ref:	449.2.17423
Medals/Awards:	1914 Star, Victory and British, plus Queen's South Africa Medal

Additional Information:

The 1891 Census showed William, aged 9, living with his mother in London Road, New Quarrington, Lincolnshire. She was the head of the household and worked as a laundress.

William enlisted into the Lincolnshire Regiment on 17th March 1900 and served as a baker for 8 years. He spent nearly a year in St. Helena in 1902 before returning to the UK. He then moved to Ireland in May 1907 until March 1908 when he transferred into the Reserves.

The 1911 Census showed William worked as a labourer but in 1912 he applied to re-join and his postal address was given as the Church Army Homes, Stockport.

William embarked for France on 12th August 1914. He was sent, dangerously ill, to Northampton Hospital on 8th June 1915, and died there five days later.

His belongings were sent to his sister Mrs Ann Clark Freeman, Gladstone Cottage, Morton, Gainsborough Lincs. The Independent reported that "..... following the hearse were Mr and Mrs Morton of Gainsborough the sister and brother-in-law of the deceased." Only one sister, Ann, was found for William and it could be that the Independent mixed where they lived with their surname.

Family:

William had four siblings, George, Elizabeth, Ann and Robert.

Courtesy of Doug Goddard

Castle Station, Northampton 1913

Sidney John COMBER

Nationality:	British
Rank:	Private
Service No:	205419
Regiment:	The Queen's (Royal West Surrey)
Unit:	3/4th Battalion
Age at Death:	19
Date of Death:	23rd February 1918
Place of Death:	Cheltenham Registration District
Parents:	Alfred Thomas and Sarah Ann Comber (nee Howes)
Address:	91 Victoria Promenade, Northampton
Grave Ref:	447.3.17372

Additional Information:

The 1901 Census showed Sidney living with his parents at Wood Leys, Roade, and that his father was a farmer. This information was repeated on the 1911 Census. The description of his funeral in The Independent stated that Sidney joined the forces in 1916 and went to France in May 1917. His brother was also serving in the forces.

Family:

Sidney had two siblings, Alfred George and Annie.

William Tait COMLEY

Nationality:	British
Rank:	Rifleman
Service No:	TR/13/64109
Regiment:	King's Royal Rifle Corps
Unit:	53rd Battalion
Age at Death:	18
Date of Death:	31st October 1918
Place of Death:	Northampton
Parents:	George and Elizabeth Bruce Comley (nee Tait)
Address:	1 Upper Dunbar Street, Wick, Caithness
Grave Ref:	463.1.17966

Additional Information:

The data collection 'Soldiers who Died In the Great War' states that William enlisted at Ipswich and resided at Alderton, Suffolk. The 53rd (Young Soldiers) Battalion was a basic recruit training unit based at Northampton. It was part of 4th Reserve Brigade.

The Northampton Daily Chronicle stated that William came from Alderton, Woodbridge, Suffolk and died at Dallington Voluntary Aid Detachment Hospital (see page 84). He died of pneumonia.

Family:

William was born on 18th September 1900 at Pulteneytown, Wick, Caithness. His father was a coastguard and previously was a Petty Officer in the Royal Navy. His parents were married on 6th May 1899.

Samuel Robert COOKE

Nationality:	Australian
Rank:	Lance Corporal
Service No:	664/A
Regiment:	Australian Infantry
Unit:	41st Battalion
Age at Death:	33
Date of Death:	4th November 1918
Place of Death:	Northampton
Parents:	Henry and Nancy Cooke (deceased)
Grave Ref:	446.2.17323
Medals/Awards:	Victory and British

Additional Information:

Samuel was born in Buckingham, Quebec, Canada, in July 1885. He enlisted on 6th January 1917 in Brisbane, Queensland into the 11th Machine Gun Corps. He left Australia on 21st June 1917 arriving at Liverpool and went to Larkhill Training Camp. He was moved to France on 27th December 1917 arriving in Rouelles. He was then moved to the 41st Battalion and appointed Lance Corporal.

He was wounded in action on 29th September 1918. He received shrapnel wounds to his right arm, lungs and heart and developed gas gangrene in his wounds. When Samuel arrived at Duston he was in a very poor condition and his right arm was amputated. He died of complications to his condition.

In his will Samuel left his estate to his brother-in-law Alf Standen, 452 Jackson Street West, Hamilton, Ontario, Canada.

Family:

Samuel had three brothers, Daniel, Harry and Thomas and two sisters who were only described as Mrs Standen and Mrs H Ramstead.

Ernest Edward COPE

Nationality:	British
Rank:	Lance Corporal
Service No:	9100
Regiment:	Wiltshire Regiment (Duke of Edinburgh's)
Unit:	1st Battalion
Age at Death:	19
Date of Death:	1st October 1915
Place of Death:	Northampton
Parents:	Frederick and Lizzie Cope
Grave Ref:	449.2.17419
Medals/Awards:	1915 Star, Victory, British

Additional Information:

Ernest was born in Newark, Lincolnshire in the autumn of 1897. The 1901 Census showed Ernest living with his parents at 13 Milton Road, Acton, London and that his father was a brick burner. They were lodging with his uncle and aunt, Walter and Mary Cope and their three children. In 1911 Ernest Edward Cope was in the Wiltshire Reformatory School, Warminster. A report in the Northampton Daily Echo at the time of his death stated that Ernest lived with his aunt and uncle, Mr and Mrs Sanderson.

Ernest enlisted at Devizes, Wiltshire and went to France on 11th August 1915.

The Independent reported that both his parents were deceased at the time of his death. The Northampton Daily Echo reported "Ernest had come to Northampton on an ambulance train and had died after his leg was amputated. His funeral was with full military honours".

Family:

The 1901 Census showed an older brother Frederick (born 1895). The report of his funeral mentioned that a grandmother, Mrs Brewitt of Lincolnshire, and his uncle and aunt, Mr and Mrs Sanderson of Lincoln, were present.

A Frederick William Cope, whose details match Ernest's older brother, is recorded on the Commonwealth War Graves Commission site as Private No.15966, 6th Battalion, Lincolnshire Regiment, buried at Philosophe British Cemetery, Mazingarbe. He died on 15th April 1918. This cemetery has casualties from the Battle of Loos but was also used to reinter others buried in isolated graves. Of the 1996 burials, 277 are unidentified.

One of a series of badges carved into the hillside above Fovant, Wiltshire during the First World War. The valley below was used as a large military camp for various regiments on their way to and from France. For more information www.fovantbadges.com

Arthur Edward COSFORD

Nationality:	British
Rank:	Warrant Officer Class II (CSM)
Service No:	5888333
Regiment:	The Queen's Royal Regiment (West Surrey)
Unit:	1/7th Battalion
Age at Death:	31
Date of Death:	3rd October 1947
Place of Death:	Northampton
Parents:	Joseph A and Winifred Ruth Cosford (nee Poole)
Grave Ref:	17265

Additional Information:

Relevant birth registration appears to be the June quarter of 1916 in Northampton.

The Northampton Daily Chronicle reported that Arthur passed away peacefully at 42 London Road. The article mentions Arthur's three siblings plus two other names, Noel and David. We have been unable to trace the relationship of these persons to Arthur.

Family:

Arthur had three siblings, Victor (born 1919), Sybil (1922) and Audrey (1925).

Thomas George COWELL

Nationality:	British
Rank:	Private 2nd Class
Service No:	305220
Regiment:	Royal Air Force
Age at Death:	24
Date of Death:	30th October 1918
Place of Death:	RAF Hospital, Tarrant, Monkton
Parents:	William and Matilda Cowell
Wife:	Ada Elizabeth Cowell, (nee Cockeril)
Address:	85 Grafton Street, Northampton
Grave Ref:	446.4.17325
Medals/Awards:	Victory and British

Additional Information:

Thomas was recorded as having been born on 11th February 1894. His mother was shown as a widow on the 1911 Census.

Thomas was a junior porter according to the 1908 UK Railway Employment Records for the London and North Western Railway at Northampton Station.

He married Ada on 25th December 1917 at the Wesleyan Methodist Chapel, Regent Square, Northampton and his stated occupation was railway shunter.

Thomas appeared before the Military Service Tribunal in June 1918. He gave his age as 24 and his address as 44 Thirlestone Road, Northampton. He said he was a porter/shunter/guard at Castle Station (now Northampton Station). He claimed deferment on the grounds that serious hardship would ensue if he was called up and he was given a temporary exemption until 15th September 1918. Case no. N9588.

Thomas died of pneumonia at Blandford Camp Hospital, Dorset.

Family:

The 1901 Census showed that he had seven siblings, Frederick, Arthur W, Herbert J, Percy, Albert Victor, Frank and George.

Percy served as Serjeant No. 5289, in the 59th Company of the Machine Gun Corps, and died on 9th February 1918. He was buried at Lijssenthoek Military Cemetery, Belgium.

Frank served as Sapper No. 526225, in the 94th Field Company of the Royal Engineers, and died on 14th April 1918. He was also buried at Lijssenthoek Military Cemetery.

Lissenthoek Military Cemetery contains 9,901 Commonwealth War Graves from the First World War of which only 24 are unidentified. There are 883 other nationalities, mostly French and German of which 11 are unidentified. There is one non World War burial.

Frederick COX

Nationality: British
Rank: Rifleman
Service No: 69486
Regiment: King's Royal Rifle Corps
Age at Death: 45 (according to death registration)
Date of Death: 23rd June 1919
Place of Death: Northampton
Address: 93 Semilong Road, Northampton
Grave Ref: 445.2.17299
Medals/Awards: Queens Sudan Medal (1896-1898)
Khedive's Sudan Medal (1896-1908
Queen's South Africa Medal with clasps,
Laing's Nek, Transvaal, Relief of Ladysmith,
Tugela Heights, King's South Africa Medal –
clasp 1901-1902

Additional Information:

Fred's medal card lists his South Africa war medals and an alternate service number, Rifle Brigade No. 2893. Apart from this, and the newspaper report, nothing can be found for Fred.

The Northampton Daily Echo reported that "Fred Cox of 93 Semilong Road, aged 43, died suddenly at the Peacock Hotel on Monday night. He left home at 9.30 pm on Monday and met Minnie Swan and went into town. When near the Peacock he said he felt ill and was taken inside the Hotel where he died at 10.15 pm. He had been demobilised from the Rifle Brigade 4 days previous. Enlisted on 18th August 1914 and had been stationed in Kingsthorpe, Northampton. He was a journeyman plasterer by trade. He had suffered with his chest and his death was attributed to valvular disease of the heart. Police found an address of his wife Mrs A Cox living at 578 Kings Road, Fulham but enquiries could find no trace of her at this address."

Lyle Hampden COX

Nationality:	Australian
Rank:	Lance Corporal
Service No:	4761
Regiment:	Australian Infantry
Unit:	58th Battalion
Age at Death:	27
Date of Death:	16th November 1918
Place of Death:	Northampton
Parents:	Rev. William and Elizabeth Cox (nee Scott)
Address:	Nagambie, Victoria, Australia
Grave Ref:	463.1.17954
Medals/Awards:	Victory and British

Additional Information:

Lyle was born in Barnedowne, Victoria, Australia and was shown on his attestation papers as a Natural Born British Subject. He worked as a milk receiver before joining-up. Lyle enlisted on 8th September 1915 in Melbourne and was nearly 24 at the time. He embarked from Australia on 7th March 1916, on board the Her Majesty's Australian Transport [HMAT] Wiltshire (see photograph page 60) and reached Suez on 10th May 1916 and eventually Marseilles, France on 30th June 1916. He then joined the 58th Battalion at Étaples.

He was admitted to hospital in France on 22nd September 1916 and was transferred to Weymouth on 22nd November 1916. He then caught mumps in February 1917, but sailed from Southampton to Le Havre on 20th June 1917 and moved to Étaples. On 6th October 1917 he was again admitted to hospital and diagnosed with shell shock. A few days before being admitted to hospital he had been promoted to Lance Corporal.

He was sent to the UK on 15th March 1918, but returned to action and was wounded with a gunshot to his right arm and chin. In addition he had jaundice. One document showed that this was his second occasion of being wounded. On 9th September 1918, he arrived in Duston, Northampton but died of wounds on 16th November 1918. He was buried at Towcester Road, on 21st November 1918.

Family:

As stated above his father was the Rev. William Cox and his mother was Elizabeth. In his will, Lyle stated his father was Presbyterian Minister of Kyabram. Lyle had a sister Ethel May.

Lyle had a brother, Private Graham Rodgers Cox, Service No. 2567, 15th Machine Gun Corps who was killed in action on 30th July 1916 and was buried at Rue de Bois.

A record of Lyle's funeral stated that his brother William Bramwell Cox sent a beautiful wreath. William was sent to Duston War Hospital on 28th October 1918, and was still a patient at the time of Lyle's death. William suffered from shell shock and was returned to Australia in January 1919, and discharged on 29th March 1919.

Lyle's third brother Hubert Franklin enlisted in June 1918. His father agreed to his enlistment as long as he was accepted for non-combatant duties. He had been assured that this was the case. Franklin survived the war, being discharged on 2nd December 1918.

Courtesy of the Australian National Archive
HMAT Wiltshire

Walter Charles Ebden COX

Nationality:	Australian
Rank:	Private
Service No:	852
Regiment:	Australian Infantry AIF
Unit:	24th Battalion
Age at Death:	32
Date of Death:	22nd September 1916
Place of Death:	War Hospital Duston
Parents:	Frederick Arthur Cox and Charlotte Barwise Cox
Address:	Pearson Street, Sale, Gippsland, Victoria
Grave Ref:	466.1.18070
Medals/Awards:	1915 Star, Victory and British

AUSTRALIAN WAR MEMORIAL

Additional Information:

Walter enlisted between 20th and 29th March 1915 at Bairnsdale, Victoria and stated his occupation was a labourer. He gave his next of kin as his mother Charlotte as his father was dead. He was born in Sale, Victoria and had previously been a member of the Rangers. He embarked on SS Euripides on 8th May 1915 heading for Gallipoli and disembarked in Alexandria on 19th January 1916.

He was then shipped to Marseilles landing on 26th March 1916. He was admitted to 2nd Canadian Stationary Hospital on 7th August 1916, with a gunshot wound to the spine and paralysis of his legs. He was moved through Boulogne on 14th August 1916 to Duston and never recovered from his wounds.

Family:

Walter had four sisters and three brothers.

One of his brothers Ernest Percival enlisted in September 1915 but never left Australia. He was diagnosed with tuberculosis and treated in Army hospitals and sanatoriums and discharged from the army on 12th August 1916. He died on 17th July 1934.

The other two brothers, Albert Henry and Frederick Daniel cannot be traced in the war records at the Australian Archives.

Walter's sisters were Ellen, Grace, Amy and Maud.

The original headstone for Walter Cox. The wording reads: "In memory of Pte W E C Cox 24th Battalion. Australian Imperial Forces. Died of wounds received in the battle of the Somme Sep. 22 1916. Aged 33 years. He rose, responsive to his Empire's call and gave his strength, his life, his all. Greater love hath no man. Erected by his relatives and comrades."

Clarence William CURTIS

Nationality:	Canadian
Rank:	Private
Service No:	255
Regiment:	Royal Canadian Dragoons
Age at Death:	20
Date of Death:	28th July 1916
Place of Death:	Northampton
Parents:	Charles William and Susie Curtis (nee Tomlin)
Address:	227 10th Street East, North Vancouver
Grave Ref:	448.4.17405
Medals/Awards:	Victory and British

Additional Information:

Clarence was born in Winnipeg, Manitoba on 1st August 1895. On his attestation papers he stated he worked as a banker and gave his mother as his next of kin. Clarence's father had died in 1901. He enlisted at Valcartier on 25th September 1914.

The Northampton Daily Echo reported that Clarence died of nephritis and that his family lived in Manitoba. The Northampton Depot supplied bugles, carriers and the firing party. Mourners included Canadian comrades, nurses and, representing the family, Mr W and Mrs H L Tomlin of Notting Hill, London.

Family:

Clarence's father died when he was about 6 years old. He and his brother Howard lived with their Aunt Mary Jane Hall (nee Tomlin) and her husband Thomas at the time of the 1906 Canadian Census. The Mr W and Mrs H L Tomlin mentioned in the report of Clarence's funeral are his Aunt Harriet Lavinia Tomlin and her son William.

Clarence's brother, Howard Winfred, served as Private No. 425766 in the 8th Battalion of the Canadian Infantry and died on 28th November 1916 on Vimy Ridge. He was buried at Lapugnoy Military Cemetery. A report of his death stated "He was seriously wounded by a bomb near

63

enemy lines. He was carried back to our own trenches where he was attended to but died on the way to a dressing station".

Clarence's mother re-married in 1918 and died in 1964.

VALCARTIER—SECTION OF THE CAMP

Valcartier Camp, Toronto, Canada

Percy Mordecai DAWSON

Nationality:	British
Rank:	Serjeant
Service No:	47225
Regiment:	Royal Scots
Unit:	1/10th Battalion
Age at Death:	32
Date of Death:	19th February 1919
Place of Death:	Ballinrobe Registration District, Ireland
Parents:	Mordecai and Mary Ann Dawson (nee Smith)
Address:	37 Perry Street, Northampton
Wife:	Ida Pearson (formerly Dawson and nee Carpenter)
Address:	85 St Nicholas Road, Great Yarmouth
Grave Ref:	445.3.17308
Medals/Awards:	Victory and British

Additional Information:

There is a record of a Percy Mordecai Dawson being christened at Holcot on 6th February 1887. On the 1891 Census he lived with his parents at 7 Margaret Street, Northampton. On the 1901 Census he lived at 37 Perry Street, Northampton aged 14 and worked as a clicker. His parents are shown as Mordecai and Mary Ann Dawson. His sister Eveline, aged 16 was still at home and worked as a machinist in the shoe trade.

On the 1911 Census Percy still lived with his parents and another sister Dorothy Irene, aged 6, at 37 Perry Street, Northampton. He was shown as a Music Hall Artiste.

The Northampton Daily Echo reported that Percy died of pneumonia at Ballinrobe, County Mayo.

Family: There is a marriage to an Ida M Carpenter in the September quarter 1912, in Northampton and a child Elizabeth M born in the December quarter 1915.

Walter James DAY

Nationality:	British
Rank:	Lance Corporal
Service No:	9208
Regiment:	Northamptonshire Regiment
Unit:	3rd Battalion
Age at Death:	25
Date of Death:	3rd February 1918
Place of Death:	Tunbridge Wells
Parents:	Walter George and Eliza Day (nee Underwood)
Address:	27 Exeter Road, Northampton
Grave Ref:	464.1.18018
Medals/Awards:	1914 Star with clasp, Victory and British

Additional Information:

The 1901 Census showed that Walter lived with his parents and six siblings at 8 Ethel Street, Northampton. His father was a cab driver. Walter was born in Northampton.

The 1911 Census showed Walter was a Private in the 1st Northamptonshire Regiment based at South Raglan Barracks, Devonport. Walter would have moved with them in October 1913 to Blackdown. He went to France with the 1st Battalion on 13th August 1914.

Walter died at the General Hospital, Tunbridge Wells from where his body was brought home for burial.

Lance Corporal Day could be the footballer who played for the 1st Battalion in 1913, and for the 1st Battalion against the 5th Battalion on 23rd January 1915 in France.

Family: Walter's siblings were Herbert (born 1886), John G (1888), Alfred (1890), Mary E (1896), William T (1899) and Albert E (1901). We are unable to determine whether any of Walter's brothers served in the First World War.

Frederick George DEACON

Nationality:	British
Rank:	Private
Service No:	4669
Regiment:	Royal Army Medical Corps
Age at Death:	30
Date of Death:	27th March 1919
Place of Death:	Northampton
Parents:	Arthur William and Annie J Deacon (nee Mansfield)
Grave Ref:	462.1.17942
Medals/Awards:	Victory and British

Additional Information:

There is a record of a Frederick George born in the December quarter 1889, in Northampton, and possibly a marriage in 1911 but no children have been found.

The 1891 Census showed him living at 37 Craven Street, Northampton, with his grandparents John and Sarah Mansfield, his mother Annie J Deacon and his siblings William J Deacon (aged 6) and Arthur J (aged 4).

The 1901 Census showed Frederick lived in the Northampton Workhouse with his younger brother Thomas aged 10. There are records for the death of an Annie J Deacon in 1895, a Sarah Mansfield in 1894 and a John Mansfield in March 1901.

The Admissions and Discharge Book for the Workhouse for the relevant period is not available and the first mention of Frederick and Thomas is on 12th April 1898 when the Minute Book mentions that "a Mrs Smith of Craven Street, had applied for the care of these children about to be returned to Mrs James of Alexandra Road and Mrs Jackson undertook to make enquiries and report to the Boarding Out Committee".

In August 1901 the Visiting Committee recommended that Frederick go on a month's trial to Mr Norris, shoemaker, 165 Park Road, St James with a view to an apprenticeship. It has to be presumed that this did not work as in November 1901 Frederick was sent out to work with C Cooke tailor of Great Houghton. In January 1902 Frederick was back in the Workhouse infirmary. In February of 1902 the Visiting Committee determined that Mr Cooke was not qualified to take an apprentice but he wanted to keep the lad as a servant. Apparently "the lad expressed himself satisfied with the home".

In August Frederick was returned from service with Mr Cooke and had to be examined by the medical officers as a result of having been ill-treated by his master. The medical officer felt there were no grounds for proceedings. However, Rev. Wodhause, Rector of Great Houghton had expressed a desire to take the boy and the Committee saw no objection to his doing so. There are no further mentions of Frederick in the Workhouse records.

In 1911 Frederick was based at the McGregor Barracks, Stanhope Lane, Aldershot as a Private in the Royal Army Medical Corps. No other information about Frederick's army service could be found.

Family:

Of Frederick's siblings only he and his older brother William lived to become adults. Arthur J died in 1898 (aged 12) and Thomas died in 1905 (aged 14).

The Workhouse Records show that on the 12th April 1898 it was agreed that William, who had been on trial with a Walter Mold of Rushden, should become his indentured apprentice. William was still with Walter Mold at the time of the 1901 Census. Walter Mold was a painter and plumber and William was working as a house painter.

As stated above Thomas was in the Workhouse with Frederick at the time of the 1901 Census. In June 1904 Thomas was moved to the Maryat Street Home. This is probably a spelling mistake and it should read 21 Marriott Road where there was a 'Children's Scattered Home (see note). The Workhouse records show that on 27th April 1904 Thomas was returned by his master (a confectioner) as being ill. He was transferred to the Berrywood Asylum on 28th April 1905 and died in the same year.

NOTE:

From the early 1900s workhouse children in Northampton were placed in a number of houses around the west side of the town known as scattered homes. In each home a group of children lived under the care of house-parents. The children helped with running of the home and attended local schools. The location of the homes included 95 St Michael's Road, 15 Colwyn Road, 2 Watkin Terrace, 1 Adelaide Terrace, 43 Semilong Road and 21 Marriott Road, all of which still survive as residential properties.

Northampton Union Workhouse was built in 1835 and could accommodate up to 300 inmates. Men, women and children were housed separately. As can be seen there was a separate infirmary and school. There was also a chapel on site. The building is now derelict.

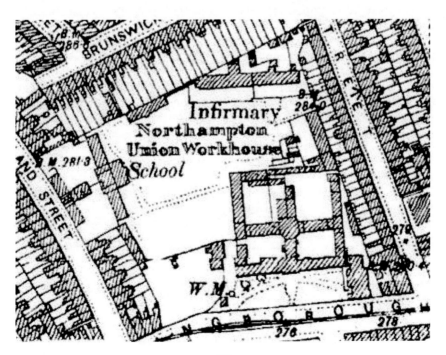

Harry DENTON

Nationality:	British
Rank:	Private
Service No:	13834
Regiments:	3rd King's Own and 4th Queen's Own Hussars
Age at Death:	43
Date of Death:	21st December 1917
Place of Death:	Northampton
Parents:	John Howe Denton and Sophia Denton
Wife:	Florence Denton
Address:	14 Bull Head Lane, Northampton
Grave Ref:	447.3.17380
Medals/Awards:	1914 Star, Victory, British, Silver War Badge No. 298522, plus the South African Medal

Additional Information:

Harry's discharge papers showed he served in the 4th Hussars, 2nd Cavalry Depot. He had previously enlisted on 14th July 1890 in Northampton. It must be assumed that Harry served in the Boer War as he received the South African Medal

Harry served at home from 26th August 1914 to 25th October 1914 when he went to France. He returned home on 14th July 1917 and was discharged on 5th September 1917 in York. Harry's pension record showed that he had heart disease, having had rheumatic fever two years previously. His medical problems are said to have been the "result of active service, exposure and strain".

The 1911 Census showed that Harry had been married to Florence for 11 years and worked as a window cleaner. They had 5 children born between 1901 and 1910. They lived at 54 Market Street, Northampton.

Family:

Harry's children were Gladys Vera (born 1901), Phyllis Gertrude (1904), William Harold (1905), Irene (1907) and Violet (1910).

Rollo Edward DIXON

The CWGC site gives his first name as Rolls but research shows that this should be Rollo

Nationality:	British
Rank:	Signalman
Service No:	2326789
Regiment:	Royal Corps of Signals
Unit:	9th Armed Division Signals
Age at Death:	18
Date of Death:	2nd December 1941
Place of Death:	Brixworth Registration District
Parents:	Arthur Charles and Amy Agnes Dixon (nee Jeffs)
Address:	Didcot, Berkshire
Grave Ref:	17267

Additional Information:

The Northampton Chronicle and Echo reported that Rollo was accidentally killed when his motor cycle was in collision with a United Counties bus at East Haddon, fracturing his skull.

Family:

There is a record of an Arthur Charles Dixon and Amy Agnes Jeffs marrying in the June quarter of 1919 with the registration district of Bedford.

Roy DOUST

Nationality:	Australian
Rank:	Private
Service No:	3558
Regiment:	Australian Infantry, A.I.F.
Unit:	54th Battalion
Age at Death:	22
Date of Death:	30th October 1916
Place of Death:	War Hospital, Duston
Parents:	William Colin Doust and the late Emily Doust (nee Apps)
Address:	Lower Southgate, Clarence River, New South Wales
Grave Ref:	465. I. 18058
Medals/Awards:	Victory and British

Additional Information:

Roy was born in 1893 in New South Wales, Australia.

Roy enlisted on 5th November 1915, at Holdsworthy, New South Wales. He was first attached to the 8/18th Battalion. He embarked for the UK on 20th December 1915, on HMAT A 60 Aeness. He transferred to the 54th Battalion at Moascar, Egypt, on 3rd April 1916. On 19th June 1916, he embarked on Hospital Transport [HT] Caledonia in Alexandria to join the British Expeditionary Force and arrived in Marseilles on 29th June 1916.

Roy was wounded in action with a gunshot wound to the chest on 19th July 1916 and embarked to the UK on H.S. St David. He was admitted to the War Hospital, Duston, on 27th July 1916.

He appeared to be recovering well and his father was sent a series of letters informing him of his son's progress. Roy was well enough during September and early October to be allowed leave in London. However, on 15th October 1916, he developed kidney problems (nephritis) and died on 30th October 1916. Roy was buried on 3rd November 1916.

Roy was 5' 8" tall, with a chest measurement of 36", with steel blue eyes and dark brown hair. He declared his religion as Methodist.

His personal effects were returned on the Barambah and his father signed for their receipt on 2nd January 1920. His personal effects consisted of 1 pocket watch (damaged), 1 Wristlet Watch with strap, 1 Mirror in Case, 1 razor, 1 clasp knife, 1 comb, 1 shaving brush, 1 purse, 1 wallet, photos, letters, 8 coins, 1 cookery book, 1 testament, 1 English-French book, 1 Fountain Pen. His pay book had been passed to the Estates Branch in London.

Family:

His parents were married in 1883 and had five children, Cecil (born 1884), Harold (1886), Elsie (1889), Roy (1893) and Arthur (1897). There are no records of any of Roy's siblings dying in the First World War.

Courtesy of Dave Humphreys

ANZAC Day Ceremony 2013

Harry Percy DOVE

Nationality:	British
Rank:	Serjeant
Service No:	T4/60539
Regiment:	Army Service Corps
Unit:	550th Horse Transport Company
Age at Death:	37
Date of Death:	16th March 1918
Place of Death:	Yarmouth Registration District
Parents:	Thomas and Elizabeth Priscilla Dove (nee Boothey)
Wife:	Maud Dove (nee Hillyard)
Address:	43 Kettering Road, Northampton
Grave Ref:	447.4.17377
Medals/Awards:	Victory and British

Additional Information:

The 1891 Census showed that Elizabeth and Harry lived with Joseph Brown who was shown as Harry's stepfather. There is a record of the death of a Thomas Dove in the June Quarter 1881 in Northampton and a marriage of Elizabeth Dove to Joseph Brown in the December quarter 1889 in Northampton

1901 Census showed Harry living with his mother at 99 St Michael's Road, Northampton. Elizabeth was working in the boot and shoe trade and Harry was shown as a last maker. The 1911 Census showed that Harry was married to Maud and they lived at 43 Kettering Road, Northampton. He was working as an engineer. His birthplace was Walworth, London.

Harry enlisted at Boxmoor in October 1914 having served five years in the Yeomanry. He died suddenly at Great Yarmouth Military Hospital, of heart failure, having been invalided back to England from Salonika.

Family: Henry had one sibling, Florence born in 1872 in Northampton. There were two children from his marriage to Maud, Frank (born 1900) and Evelyn (1908).

Charles Lewis DURLEY

Nationality:	British
Rank:	Private
Service No:	TR/13/10272
Regiment:	King's Royal Rifle Corps
Unit:	18th Battalion Training Reserve
Age at Death:	36
Date of Death:	22nd April 1917
Place of Death:	Northampton
Parents:	George and Elizabeth Durley (nee Cockell)
Address:	172 Kennington Lane, Vauxhall, London
Wife:	Emily Jessie Eliza Durley (nee Rowles)
Address:	34 Aycliffe Road, Shepherds Bush, London
Grave Ref:	448.2.17387

Additional Information:

Charles was born in Deptford, Kent. The 1901 Census showed that Charles lived with his parents and worked as an upholsterer. The 1911

Census showed that he was married to Emily and lived at 12 Renton Road, London. He still worked as an upholsterer.

Charles enlisted at Deptford in 1916. His attestation papers, which are badly damaged, showed that he and Emily had one child, also named Charles Lewis.

From the Coroner's report it would appear that he drowned in the Nene near Westley's Mill.

The Northampton Daily Echo reported that a passer-by heard a splash and someone was seen struggling in the water. A life belt was found and thrown in but the man failed to grasp it and sank beneath the water. The body was recovered and it was found to be Charles. He was billeted at College Street Church Rooms. They reported that he had been married for about 15 years and had a son. The day before he died a woman tried to see him but he refused to see her. She left a note that said "why won't you see me, as she was his wife of 14 months".

Emily and Charles were married on 2nd August 1901 and their son was born on 21st June 1904. One could wonder whether the report of "14 months" was misquoted. No second marriage can be found for Charles.

After Charles's death, his widow, Emily, was being considered for a pension. One was not granted as "the death was due to his own fault". The case was referred to another branch of the military but no outcome was found in his papers. Another document showed that his personal effects and any medals should be sent to Emily at 39 West End Lane, Hampstead, London. No medal card could be found.

Family:

Charles had a brother, George H F Durley who lived at 6 Victoria Mansions, Golders Green, London. Emily died in 1966.

James Henry DURRANT

Nationality:	British
Rank:	Private
Service No:	SD/5342
Regiment:	Royal Sussex
Unit:	14th Battalion (CWGC says 4th)
Age at Death:	21
Date of Death:	13th March 1916
Place of Death:	Northampton
Parents:	Henry and Emily Durrant (nee Wakeford)
Address:	Balls Cross, Petworth
Grave Ref:	449.4.17421

Additional Information:

The 1901 Census showed that James lived with his parents in Kirkford. His father was an agricultural labourer. The 1911 Census showed James living with his father (his mother died in 1907). His father was still working as an agricultural labourer and James was a boot maker's apprentice. His father died in 1914.

Family:

James was one of ten children and his siblings were William, Emily, George, Alfred, David, Ada, Laura, Daniel and Annie.

His brother David served as Private No. 2715 in the Royal Army Service Corps. He enlisted on 23rd September 1914 and was demobbed on 19th June 1919. He had served in France from 14th October 1914 to 18th May 1919. He received the 1914 Star, British and Victory Medals.

Daniel appears to have died in Petworth in 1915 but was not recorded as a casualty of war.

Charles Henry EALES

Nationality:	British
Rank:	Private
Service No:	28323
Regiment:	3rd Battalion, Northamptonshire
Transferred to:	Labour Corps Service No. 546153
Age at Death:	27
Date of Death:	7th November 1918
Place of Death:	Northampton (Abington Avenue Hospital)
Parents:	Charles Henry and Catherine (Kate) Eales (nee Burrows)
Address:	19 Harley Street, Stoke, Coventry (his father's address in 1918)
Grave Ref:	463.1.17962
Medals/Awards:	Victory and British

Additional Information:

Charles appeared before the Military Service Tribunal at Northampton in July 1916 giving his address as 42 Kingswell Street and his trade as milkman. His reason for appealing was that it was more in the national interest for him to do his normal job than go in the forces. His employer backed his application, the reason being "in addition to his work as a milkman he delivers milk to about 150 customers and I am unable to get other labour. Women cannot replace this man's labour." He was given a temporary exemption to 25th September 1916. The case no. was N838. (See also Reuben Pittams, brother of Arthur Ernest Pittams).

Charles joined the Northamptonshire Regiment on 9th October 1916. He was posted to the 7th Battalion in the field on 26th January 1917, and was wounded in action on 11th April 1917. He was repatriated to Huddersfield Hospital with a gunshot wound to his left shoulder and spent 76 days in hospital. After this period he was recommended for a Command Depot and was posted to Northampton in March 1918. He died of influenza which turned to pneumonia and his mother was present at his bedside.

Charles was born in Bugbrooke on 11th May 1891. The 1901 Census showed Charles living with his parents and siblings at the High Street,

Bugbrooke and his father was a waggoner. By the time of the 1911 Census Charles was living with his employer at 42 Kingswell Street, Northampton and engaged in dairy work.

Family:

Charles had nine siblings, Florence, William, Eli, Fred, John, George, Arthur, Margaret and Ernest. All of the brothers seem to have survived the First World War.

Photograph of the men who sat on the Military Tribunals 1914-1918

George Campbell EASTON

Nationality:	Australian
Rank:	Corporal
Service No:	5547 (CWGC says 554)
Regiment:	Australian Machine Gun Corps
Unit:	2nd Battalion
Age at Death:	31
Date of Death:	4th November 1918
Place of Death:	Northampton
Parents:	John Alexander and Elizabeth Easton (nee Bradley)
Address:	20 Rowley Street, Camperdown, Sydney
Grave Ref:	446.3.17320
Medals/Awards:	Victory and British

Additional Information:

George was born in Balmain, Sydney on 28th December 1887. The portrait above was signed "Yours truly George 12.1.1918". He enlisted

80

on 24th May 1916 at the Royal Australian Showground, Sydney. He had previously served in the Volunteer E Company Sydney. He gave his occupation as commercial traveller.

George left Australia via Melbourne on 6th December 1916 and arrived in Plymouth on 17th February 1917. He trained at the Machine Gun Training Depot just outside Grantham before moving to France on 6th May 1917. He was wounded in action on 4th October 1917 with a gunshot wound to the knee.

George was sent to Weymouth to convalesce and after further training he returned to France on 8th February 1918. He accidentally injured the same knee on 2nd October 1918. He was evacuated to Northampton and died of influenza and pneumonia.

Family:

He had three brothers, John, James and Alexander, and one sister Elsie Margaret. Alexander was executor to his will. James embarked for the war on 2nd November 1918 and his ship was recalled to Australia. He was discharged on 23rd December 1918.

Additional Source: Ancestry UK – Bradley Family Tree

Badge carved into the hill above Fovant, Hampshire where the Australian Forces had a large camp (see page 54)

Harold ELDRED
(known as Harry)

Nationality:	British
Rank:	Warrant Officer
Service No:	507361
Regiment:	Royal Air Force
Age at Death:	41
Date of Death:	1st September 1945
Place of Death:	Sevenoaks
Parents:	Arthur Cartwright and Lucy Eldred (nee Smith)
Wife:	Elsie Winnifred Eldred (nee Tebbutt)
Address:	58 Burder Street, Loughborough
Grave Ref:	17264

Additional Information:

The 1911 Census showed Harold lived at 58 Burder Street, Loughborough, with his parents and his father worked as a yard foreman for Midland Railways.

The Northampton Daily Chronicle reported that Harold died at Guys USA Hospital in Sevenoaks.

Family:

Harold had one sister, Doris, aged 4 at the time of the 1911 Census and a brother, Frank, who was born later that year.

Harold and Elsie had a daughter, Elsie V, born in 1944 in Northampton.

Additional Source: Ancestry UK - Charnock Family Tree

William Emanuel ELEY

Nationality:	British
Rank:	Serjeant
Service No:	G/10090
Regiment:	The Queen's (Royal West Surrey)
Unit:	3rd Battalion
Age at Death:	36 (correct age may be 44)
Date of Death:	7th August 1918
Place of Death:	Northampton
Parents:	John and Elizabeth Eley (nee Kettlewell)
Wife:	Lillian Daisy Eley (nee Wilson)
Address:	71 Weedon Road, St James, Northampton
Grave Ref:	447.2.17367

Additional Information:

The only William Emmanuel found on records was born in 1874 in Ross, Herefordshire. The 1891 Census showed that he lived with his parents at Cadogan Square, London where his father was a doorkeeper. William was working as a jeweller's clerk.

William married Adeline Christine Morrison on 19th September 1896 and they had a son William who died when he was one year old. The 1901 Census showed William and Adeline with no children living at 25 Petworth Street, Battersea, London. Adeline died in 1902. William cannot be found on the 1911 Census.

In 1909 there was a marriage for William to a Mary Gilmour in Irvin, Scotland. He gave his age as 29 which ties with his age on the death registration. His parents, given on the wedding registration, are consistent with the 1891 Census record so it would seem that at some point he decided to change his year of birth. William and Mary had a son, William Stephen, on 1st January 1912, and this son is mentioned on the pension application following his death. Mary died on 7th May 1915.

William enlisted on 22nd December 1915 in Battersea. He gave his occupation as clerk and marital status as widower. He stated he had previously served six years with the Royal Scots Fusiliers but no record of this has been found. His parents were deceased.

William married Lillian Daisy on 22nd December 1917. She made an application for a pension following his death and was awarded 16s 3d (£0.82). On the application Lillian stated that she understood that William's son, William Stephen, was living at 31 Allison Street, Merton in Ayr, Ayr, Scotland.

His record does not show him leaving the country but his cause of death seems to contradict this. He was assigned to Northampton where his second wife Lillian was living. He died of Uraemia (kidney failure) possibly due to poison gas.

Dallington Hall which was used as a Voluntary Aid Detachment Hospital

Arthur Pearson ELLIOTT

Nationality: British
Rank: Private
Regiment: Northamptonshire (22979)
Transferred to: Royal Defence Corps (5359)
Age at Death: 53
Date of Death: 5th January 1917
Place of Death: Hitchin
Wife: Sarah Annie Elliott (nee Johnson)
Address: 60 St Andrews Road, Northampton
Grave Ref: 465.1.18042

Additional Information:

At the time of the 1901 Census Arthur was living in the Barracks of the Depot of the Northamptonshire Regiment and married to Sarah. They had one child. He was a soldier with the rank of Private. The 1911 Census showed Arthur's occupation as roadman and that he was an army pensioner living in Paulerspury, Towcester. He was born in Keystone, Huntingdonshire.

The Northampton Daily Echo reported that Arthur died at a hospital in Hertfordshire. His funeral took place at St Sepulchre's Church, being given military honours with the Northampton Depot providing bearers and a firing party.

Family:

Sarah and Arthur had three daughters, Euphemia Virtue, Alberta Frederike Ruby and Edwina Maria Ivy. There was also a stepson, Percy Raymond Johnson.

William FALLA

Nationality:	British
Rank:	Private
Service No:	SE/21189
Regiment:	Army Veterinary Corps
Unit:	Depot.
Age at Death:	28
Date of Death:	5th April 1917
Place of Death:	Northampton
Parents:	Selby and Margaret Ann Falla (nee Wilkinson)
Address:	121 Thornborough Street, Byker
Grave Ref:	448.3.17392
Medals/Awards:	Victory and British

Additional Information:

William's father died in 1892. The 1901 Census showed William lived with his mother and stepfather, named as John Bradley, in Byker, Newcastle upon Tyne together with his brothers and step brothers and sisters.

The 1911 Census showed Margaret was again a widow and had reverted to the surname Falla (no marriage record could actually be traced for her marriage to John Bradley) and all the children bore the Falla surname. William worked as a labourer in a quarry. William's mother died in 1913.

The Northampton Daily Echo recorded that William's funeral took place using a gun carriage from Royal Field Artillery and the Training Reserve provided an escort and firing party. It also recorded that William died at Duston War Hospital aged 26 (this age does not tie with any other record).

Family:

William had six siblings, Selby (born 1883), Arthur (1885), John (1887), Joseph (1892), Frank (1896) and Annie (1898).

Selby was recorded on the CWGC site as Private No. 34156, King's Own Royal Lancaster Regiment who died on 25th March 1920 and was buried at Byker & Heaton Cemetery, Newcastle upon Tyne. He was awarded the 1915 Star, Victory, British and a Silver War Badge. The records for the Silver War Badge No. 682 show that Selby had his right forearm amputated and was in the Northumberland Fusiliers at the time of his discharge, on 16th August 1916, due to his wounds.

Arthur was recorded in the Royal Navy Reserves War Awards as being given an 'Approbation of services rendered' on the occasion of the rescue of the crew of the lighter "Annie" off Middlesbrough on 28th August 1917. He was awarded the Victory and British medals.

John may have served as Thomas John and been awarded the Victory and British medals.

We are unable to verify the service of Joseph or Frank.

A typical sweetheart cushion made by soldiers during WW1. This particular cushion shows the badge of the Army Veterinary Corps.

Alfred FITZHUGH

Nationality: British
Rank: Private
Regiment: Northamptonshire Regiment (No.10212)
Transferred to: Labour Corps (No. 369195)
Age at Death: 42 (40 according to year of birth)
Date of Death: 17th November 1918
Place of Death: Hammersmith Registration District
Parents: George and Kate Fitzhugh
Wife: Eliza Fitzhugh (nee Paxman)
Address: 3 Spring Lane, Northampton
Grave Ref: 446.3.17312
Medals/Awards: 1914/15 Star, Victory, British and Silver War Badge

Additional Information:

Alfred was born in Ilkeston, Derbyshire in 1878. At the time of the 1881 Census he, his parents and his siblings were living in Northampton. His father was a bricklayer's labourer.

Alfred enlisted into the Northamptonshire Regiment on 27th October 1894 as Private No. 4452 having already served in the 4th Battalion, Northamptonshire Regiment (Militia). Prior to this he had worked as a shoe finisher. He did his initial training at the Depot and on 7th January 1895 moved to the 2nd Battalion at Colchester. On 25th September he left England with a draft of one Serjeant, two Corporals and 97 men to join the 1st Battalion who were based at Secunderabad in India. They arrived on 17th October 1896.

During Alfred's time in India the 1st Battalion was based at Secunderabad in 1896, and was on campaign in 1897 on the North West Frontier (skirmishes with the Pastuns and Orakzais in the Khyber Pass). He gained the India Medal 1895 with clasps for Samana 1897 and Tirah 1897-1898.

The battalion arrived at Peshawar in April 1898 and moved to Fyzabad in June 1898. It was based at Allahabad in 1899 and 1900; Fyzabad and Umballa in November 1901. It took part in the Coronation Durbar in

1902, and then moved to Dagshai and Jullunder in 1903. Alfred returned to England in March 1903 and finished his time with the Regiment on 26th October 1906.

By the time of the 1911 Census, Alfred was living with his wife Eliza and one son, Alfred, though two further children were shown as having died. Alfred was working as a hatter and furrier and the family lived at 3 Spring Lane, Northampton. Two further children were born, Sydney in 1912 and George in 1913.

Alfred re-enlisted into the Northamptonshire Regiment on 14th August 1914, trained with the 3rd Battalion and was transferred to the 5th Pioneer Battalion. He went to France with this battalion on 29th May 1915. He was transferred later to the Eastern Command Centre (a holding centre for soldiers about to be discharged) as Private No. 36195.

He was discharged from the army on 4th June 1918 owing to sickness and given a Silver War Badge No. 395251. His pension record gave his trade as a platelayer and his intended address on discharge was 37 Southbrook Street, Shepherds Bush, London. He was said to be honest and industrious.

Alfred died of pneumonia in a London Hospital.

Family:

Alfred had nine siblings but only five, including Alfred, were alive at the time of the 1911 Census.

He married Eliza in 1904 and the 1911 Census indicates that she was disabled. Of their five children only two, Alfred and Sydney, lived beyond infancy.

Harry FROST

Nationality:	British
Rank:	Private
Regiment:	2nd Battalion, Northamptonshire (7632)
Transferred to:	Labour Corps (427092)
Age at Death:	30
Date of Death:	17th December 1918
Place of Death:	Northampton
Parents:	Emma Frost
Wife:	Ethel Florence Frost (nee Barker)
Address:	7 West Street, Northampton
Grave Ref:	445.4.17309
Medals/Awards:	1914 Star and clasp, Victory and British

Additional Information:

Service No. 7632 was issued to Harry in about 1906 and he would have been a regular soldier. He could have been serving with the 1st Battalion in August 1914 or called up with the reserves. No service or pension record could be found. According to Harry's medal card he went to France on 13th August 1914 and the clasp indicates he served in the front line.

Family:

A family tree on Ancestry gives his parents as Emma and William. Harry appears to have married Ethel Florence in 1916 and a son, Ronald Sydney, was born in 1916.

Additional Source: Ancestry UK – Mundin Family Tree

Walter Thomas GARDNER

Nationality: British
Rank: Private
Service No: 4168
Regiment: Northamptonshire
Unit: 4th Battalion
Age at Death: 51
Date of Death: 15th January 1916
Place of Death: Northampton
Parents: Thomas and Sarah Gardner
Wife: Emma Gardner (nee Walmsley)
Address: 15 Artizan Road, Northampton
Grave Ref: 448.3.17416

Additional Information:

Walter was born in 1865 to Thomas and Sarah Gardner.

In 1874, in the Minute Book of the Towcester Workhouse, there was a reference to Walter. He was asking for readmission due to having been 'severely beaten'. He would have been aged nine at the time.

His father, Thomas died before the 1881 Census and Sarah was living with her sister and brother in law and stated she was a widow. One of the children was living with an uncle and none of the other children, including Walter, can be found on the 1881 Census.

Walter joined the Duke of Cornwall's Light Infantry on 15th July 1882. He was in Ireland from 19th September 1883 to 10th October 1884. He was then sent to Malton between 17th December 1885 and 26th February 1888. In February 1886 Walter was hospitalised with jaundice and again in March 1886 with a strangulated hernia. In December 1886 he was imprisoned for 15 days for "inflicting bodily harm". He was discharged with a note that his conduct was "bad and his habits rather intemperate".

The papers for his time in the Duke of Cornwall's Light Infantry include a handwritten reference to the 3rd Battalion Northamptonshire Regiment (see below).

The 1891 Census showed Walter married to Emma and working as a shoe riveter. They lived at South Place, Towcester.

In July 1901 Emma was in the workhouse with her children, Elsie, Walter, James, Ellen and Florence. Emma was described as "married, living apart, pregnant and destitute". They were all discharged at their own request on 14th July 1901.

In December 1906 there was a letter in the Visiting Committee book of the Workhouse from a G Whitney of Oxford. He stated that "Walter Gardener was no longer in his employ but that he had seen him in town. He told Mr Whitney that he was getting a bit of work but barely a living for him and he told me if he worked hard he could earn 15s (£0.75) a week. He told me that he was in trouble as he was to allow his wife 12s.6d (£0.52½) per week and I feel sorry for him as I know that he can't carry it and I thought that by the way he spoke to me he was coming up to meet you".

Walter appeared before the Committee on 13th December 1906 to discuss his position regarding his wife and the charge and warrant against himself. The Committee, after hearing him, suggested that he endeavour to accept responsibility by 2nd week in January.

The next mention in the Workhouse records was on 19th November 1908, when he was admitted and his circumstances were described as "married living apart destitute and ruptured". He left on 20th January 1909, at his own request.

By the 1911 Census Thomas lived as a boarder in Northampton and Emma lived with the children at 6 Uppingham Road, Northampton.

The Commonwealth War Grave record stated that Walter served in the South African Campaign but this cannot be verified. However, there is a record of a W Gardner, Private No. 6396 in the 3rd Battalion Northamptonshire Regiment in the Boer War gaining the Queens Medal with clasp for Cape Colony and South Africa 1902.

Family:

Walter and Emma married in 1891 and had ten children: Elsie, Walter, James, Ellen, Florence, Sarah, Charles, Abigail, Grace and Joseph.

James served as Staff Serjeant No. 72207 with the 134th Field Ambulance of the Royal Army Medical Corps 134th Field Ambulance. He joined in Kettering in October 1915. He married Emily on 15th February 1916 in Fleet and embarked for France on 6th March 1916. He died of wounds received in the field on 4th September 1916, and is buried at Acheux British Cemetery (see picture below).

Acheux British Cemetery, France
There are 180 burials, all from the First World War
James is buried in Row A, which contains casualties from the
Battle of The Somme, in July, August and September 1916

James Fleming GARNER

Nationality:	British
Rank:	Private
Service No:	3/11101
Regiment:	Northamptonshire
Unit:	6th Battalion
Age at Death:	32
Date of Death:	11th October 1918
Place of Death:	Guildford
Parents:	James Bliss and Annie Garner (nee Fleming)
Address:	14 Silver Street, Northampton
Grave Ref:	446.2.17327
Medals/Awards:	1914 Star and clasp, Victory and British

Additional Information:

James was baptised on 24th July 1887 in Wootton. The 1901 Census showed that he lived with his Uncle James and worked as a painter. By the 1911 Census James was living with his parents at Preston Deanery, Northampton and worked as a farm labourer.

James's medal card showed that he entered the theatre of war on 12th November 1914. He went to France with a draft of the 1st Battalion Northamptonshire Regiment. Sometime later he transferred to the 6th Battalion Northamptonshire Regiment. He died of wounds at Clandon Park, Guildford.

He was buried, after a service held at St Sepulchre's Church, with full military honours with escort, buglers, bearers, firing party and gun carriage provided by Brigade HQ.

Family:

James had six siblings, Thomas, Annie, Agnes, Catherine, Jane and Dorothy.

Glendon Kenneth GARRETT
(known as Glen)

Nationality:	British
Rank:	Private
Service No:	14358115
Regiment:	General Service Corps
Age at Death:	34
Date of Death:	21st April 1943
Place of Death:	Chesterfield
Parents:	William Charles and Alice Maud (nee Rabbitt)
Wife:	Phyllis Laura Garrett (nee Hillyer)
Address:	31 Briar Hill Road, Northampton
Grave Ref:	17910

Additional Information:

Glen was born in Northampton in 1908. The 1911 Census showed he lived with his parents at 20 Alpha Street, Northampton and his father was a boot finisher.

In his will Glen left an estate worth £505 to his widow.

His headstone commemorates his wife Phyllis Laura Garrett, 1909-1996.

Family:

Glen had six siblings, Alice, Ethel, Gertrude, Hilda Rose, Douglas and Joan. He had two daughters, Betty and Dorothy.

William Thomas GASCOIGNE

Nationality:	British
Rank:	Private
Regiment:	Royal Army Medical Corps (96400)
Transferred to:	King's Liverpool Regiment (80213)
Unit:	Labour Companies Depot (Oswestry)
Age at Death:	22
Date of Death:	11th June 1917
Place of Death:	Oswestry Registration District
Parents:	Thomas and Mary Elizabeth Gascoigne (nee Webb)
Address:	Culworth
Grave Ref:	445.17283

Additional Information:

William was born in Culworth, around 1895. The 1901 Census showed that William lived with his parents in Culworth. His father was a blacksmith. The 1911 Census again showed William living with his parents in Culworth and his occupation was given as 'blacksmith's son working in a shop'. He enlisted in Northampton.

William is buried in the Baptist Chapel Yard, Culworth (now a private house) with a memorial gravestone in Towcester Road Cemetery.

By March 1917, the 23rd and 24th (Works) Battalions, Liverpool Regiment, became the 1st Labour Battalion, Labour Corps, in 1917, and was based in Hereford.

Family:

William had a sister, Ivy, but she died in infancy before the 1911 Census.

William Edward GOACHER

Nationality:	British
Rank:	Private
Service No:	05728
Regiment:	Royal Army Ordnance Corps [RAOC]
Unit:	41st Company
Age at Death:	37
Date of Death:	3rd January 1917
Place of Death:	Registered Daventry
Parents:	William and Ellen Goacher (nee Richardson)
	177 Clarendon Road, Notting Hill, London
Wife:	Polly Goacher (nee Arnold)
Address:	177 Clarendon Road, Notting Hill West, London
Grave Ref:	465.1.18046
Medals/Awards:	1915 Star, Victory and British

Additional Information:

William was born in Hove, Sussex around 1879. In 1911 William lived in Notting Hill West and his occupation was a house painter. He enlisted in Shepherd's Bush, Middlesex.

William landed in France with RAOC on 7th October 1915. The task of the RAOC was the maintenance and repair of armaments and munitions.

The Northampton Daily Echo reported that William, a native of London, died from pneumonia at Daventry Auxiliary Hospital. He was given a funeral with military honours and relatives from London attended.

Family:

William had two daughters, Gladys and Barbara.

William GOODSALL

Nationality:	British
Rank:	Private
Regiment:	10th London Regiment (No. 20616)
Transferred to:	Royal Defence Corps (No. 3410)
Unit:	66th Provisional Company
Age at Death:	52
Date of Death:	6th January 1918
Place of Death:	Northampton
Wife:	Charlotte Caroline Goodsall (nee Parker)
Address:	10 Wellington View, Hough Lane, Leyland, Lancs
Grave Ref:	447.2.7379

Additional Information:

There is a mystery about where William was born, as the 1901 Census showed Gravesend but the 1911 listed Dalston. There are possible birth records for both places. However, it seems clear that William married a Charlotte Caroline Parker in 1893 and the 1901 Census showed they lived in Edmonton where he worked as a painter. By the time of the 1911 Census they lived with a cabinet maker, Charles Aldridge and family at 61 Winchester Road, Lower Edmonton. William was working as a painter decorator.

William enlisted in Hackney and it is unlikely that he left the Home Theatre. William died of pneumonia.

Family:

The 1911 Census showed that William and Caroline had two children both living but not with them. A Susan Rebecca (born 1905 in Edmonton) has been confirmed as their child but on the 1911 Census no record of her or the other sibling can be found. The family tree shows that Susan lived to have a family of her own.

Additional Sources: Ancestry UK - Thompsom family tree

Marian GORZKIEWICZ

Nationality:	Polish
Rank:	Sergeant
Service No:	30036845
Regiment:	Polish Resettlement Corps
Unit:	See below
Age at Death:	28
Date of Death:	19th November 1947
Place of Death:	Northampton
Parents:	Stefan and Maria Gorzkiewicz (Horbowska)
Address:	Zagórze 197, Dolina, county of Stanislawów, Poland (now Ukraine)
Grave Ref:	17279
Medals/Awards:	British: 1939-45 Star, Italy Star, Defence Medal War Medal 1939-45 Polish: Bronze Cross of Merit with swords, Cross of Monte Cassino No. 4732, Army Medal

Additional Information:

Prior to the start of the Second World War Marian worked as an apprentice locksmith.

In September 1939 Marian's home was occupied by the former Soviet Union. Being of Polish nationality, he was deported and held in the former Soviet Union but details of where and how long are not known.

On 30th July 1941 an agreement called the 'Sikorski-Maisky' was completed and Marian was released for the purpose of joining the Polish Armed Forces, which were being organised in 1941-42 on the territory of the former USSR. He enlisted in the Polish Army on 22nd March 1942 and was posted to 10 Anti-Aircraft Artillery Battery, 10 Infantry Division.

Together with the Polish Army units they crossed the Soviet-Iranian border and came under British command, with effect from 1st April 1942. Via Iraq, he was transferred to Palestine, where he arrived on 29th April 1942 and was posted to the Reserve of the Commander-in-Chief, Polish Army Middle East.

On the re-organisation of the Polish Army in the Middle East he was transferred to 3 Light Anti-Aircraft Artillery Regiment, 3 Carpathian Infantry Division, 2 Polish Corps, 8 British Army on 14th November 1942.

Marian served in Iran, Iraq, Palestine and Egypt in 1942 through 1943 and in Italy from 1943 to 1946 when, together with 2 Polish Corps, he was transferred to the UK. Due to a gradual demobilisation of the Polish Forces under British command, Marian enlisted in the Polish Resettlement Corps.

Marian served in actions on the Rivers Sangro and Rapido/Southern Apennines; battle for Monte Cassino Gustav-Hitler line of enemy defences; battle for Ancona/Goths line of enemy defences; helped the rear-guard of 8th British Army and actions in the Northern Apennines, River Senio and the battle for Bologna/Lombardy Plain.

Photograph of 2nd Polish Corps in Italy courtesy of the Kresy-Siberia Virtual Museum. www.kresy-siberia.org

Nathan HAMER

Nationality:	British
Rank:	Lance Serjeant
Service No:	10001
Regiment:	Northamptonshire Regiment
Unit:	5th Battalion
Age at Death:	24
Date of Death:	3rd February 1918
Place of Death:	West Derby Registration District
Parents:	Hector J and Hannah Hamer (nee Wortley)
Address:	6 Fetter Street, Northampton
Grave Ref:	447.2.17375
Medals/Awards:	1915 Star, Victory and British

Additional Information:

Nathan was born around 1895 at Oldbury, Worcs. In 1911 he lived at 6 Fetter Street, Northampton with his parents and three brothers (two more siblings were living away). His father was an iron moulder.

Nathan worked as a photographer's assistant. He was employed by Henry Cooper and Sons before the War.

Nathan enlisted at Northampton. The 5th (Service) Battalion Northants Regiment was formed at Northampton in August 1914, part of K1 12th (Eastern) Division. In January 1915 it became a Pioneer Battalion, and landed in France on 30th May 1915. Nathan was wounded on 30th November 1917. In his book about the 5th Battalion, Geoffrey Moore states "the 5th Battalion were thrown into the front line at Cambrai and A Company were heavily engaged when the Germans attacked and the company retired to near the Revelon Farm, Gouzeaucourt Road where, with the 11th Middlesex on the left, a stand was made until Cavalry came up to reinforce".

Nathan had been at the front for two years at the time of his death.

Family:

Nathan was the younger brother of Hector, Arthur, Albert and Ernest and older brother of Frank. Four of the brothers also served.

Sources:

Northampton Independent article and photo, 9th February 1918 *Kitchener's Pioneers – The Story of the 5th Battalion,* page 27, by Geoffrey Moore

George William HANCOCK

Nationality:	British
Rank:	Private
Service No:	M/377321
Regiment:	Army Service Corps
Unit:	373rd Mechanised Transport Company
Age at Death:	26
Date of Death:	16th October 1918
Place of Death:	Northampton
Parents:	William and Annie Hancock (nee Parker)
Wife:	E E Hancock
Address:	45 Wilby Street, Northampton
Grave Ref:	446.4.17329
Medals/Awards:	1915 Star, Victory and British

Additional Information:

George was born around 1893 in Ashby-de-la-Zouch. In 1901 the family were living at 15 North Street, Millbank, Ashby de la Zouch and his father was a railway labourer. The 1911 Census showed George living with his parents in Ashby de la Zouch and that he worked as a railway labourer. His father was a garden labourer. George enlisted in Ashby.

Records show that George had first served as a Lance Corporal in the 1/5th Leicester Regiment with a service number of 1194. His medal card showed he landed in France on 27th February 1915 with the 1/5th Battalion. Sometime later he transferred to the 373rd Company Army Service Corps that operated at Colchester, Bedford and Hitchin. He died of pneumonia.

Family:

The only marriage of a Hancock to someone with E E as their initials is to an Edith E Spurr in June 1911 in Sheffield. We are unable to verify if this is the right person.

Denis HAYES

Nationality:	British
Rank:	Private
Service No:	8681
Regiment:	Royal Munster Fusiliers
Unit:	3rd Battalion
Age at Death:	32
Date of Death:	4th September 1920
Place of Death:	Northampton
Grave Ref:	443.4.17297
Medals/Awards:	1914 Star, Victory and British

Additional Information:

In 1911 Denis was serving as a 21 year-old Private with 2nd Battalion Royal Munster Fusiliers at Jellalabad Military Barracks, Tidworth, Wiltshire. The census gave his birth as 1890, Coolhagen, Cork.

Denis entered the theatre of war on 13th August 1914. The 2nd and 3rd Battalions Royal Munster Fusiliers were regular army battalions. The 2nd Battalion landed in France at Le Havre on 14th August 1914 and it would appear that Denis was part of the 2nd at that time. The 2nd Battalion fought on the front throughout the war being absorbed by the 1st Battalion on 19th April 1918. The 3rd Battalion was a reserve battalion in Ireland, then England and it would appear that Denis was transferred to the 3rd at some point in his career.

The Northampton Daily Echo reported that "arrangements are being made to bury an Irish ex-soldier who died of pneumonia at the Workhouse. Denis Hayes said his mother lived in Cork but efforts to trace her have failed. He was taken to the workhouse recently."

Denis's workhouse record showed he was a labourer, Roman Catholic, born 2nd January 1898 and entered the workhouse on 3rd September 1920 and died the following day.

William HICKMAN

Nationality:	British
Rank:	Private
Regiment:	Northamptonshire Regiment (23109)
Transferred to:	Royal Defence Corps (28292)
Unit:	65th Company
Age at Death:	49
Date of Death:	12th April 1917
Place of Death:	Northampton
Address:	Northampton
Grave Ref:	448.2.17391

Additional Information:

William enlisted in Northampton.

The Northampton Daily Chronicle on 17th April 1917 recorded that his funeral was with full military honours and a gun carriage from the Royal Field Artillery was used and the Training Reserve provided an escort and firing party. It stated that William, who came from Daventry, died aged 49 at Duston War Hospital.

A William Charles Hickman born in 1868 in Daventry was recorded as living with his parents Henry and Sarah (nee Drury). On the 1891 Census William was lodged at the White Horse Inn, Daventry and worked in the shoe trade. He was still there for the 1901 Census but no trace can be found of him on the 1911 Census.

Family:

If this is the right William Hickman he had six siblings, Charlotte (born 1849), Mary (1851), Henry (1854), Sarah (1855), Rose (1860) and Annie (1863).

Harry HILLYER

Nationality:	British
Rank:	Private
Service No:	M2/150599
Regiment:	Army Service Corps
Unit:	303rd Mechanised Transport Company
Age at Death:	20
Date of Death:	9th February 1916
Place of Death:	Marlborough, Wiltshire
Parents:	Henry and Emma Hillyer (nee Cooke)
Address:	89 Southampton Road, Far Cotton, Northampton
Grave Ref:	297.3.11588

Additional Information:

Harry was born around 1896 in Northampton. On the 1901 Census Harry was shown as living with the parents, and his sister Kate, at 158 Bridge Street, Northampton. In 1911 he was a 15 year-old apprentice engineer in a motor works living with his parents and siblings at 15 Cotton End, Northampton. His father was a blacksmith.

106

He enlisted on 22nd November 1915 in London. He was still living with his parents but they had moved to the address above. He worked as a motor fitter. Before enlisting Harry had been apprenticed with Messrs Johnson Wrights, Northampton and was working in Luton.

The 303rd Mechanised Transport Company of the Army Service Corps was within the 35th Division of the Army Service Corps. It was mainly composed of locally raised "bantam" troops, i.e. men below the regulation height of 5' 3". From August 1915 it was based on Salisbury Plain with Headquarters at Marlborough. Harry served as a motor fitter.

Harry died "in his billet" in Marlborough, Wilts, on 9th February 1916 and an inquest was held. He had apparently been vaccinated some weeks before and developed a painful arm, which had put him off duty. On the day he resumed duty he complained to his comrades that he was feeling cold. When his comrades returned from their supper he was found dead in a chair in front of the fire. The verdict was "death from natural causes due to heart failure owing to disease of the heart, aggravated by lung trouble".

No medal card could be found. However, a document in his service papers showed that his personal effects, and any medals due, should be sent to his father Henry Hillyer.

Family:

Harry had three siblings, Kate (born 1893), Emma (1902) and William (1904).

Ronald HOLLOWAY
(known as Chick)

Nationality:	British
Rank:	Aircraftman 2nd Class
Service No:	944357
Regiment:	Royal Air Force Volunteer Reserve [RAFVR]
Age at Death:	23
Date of Death:	25th April 1940
Place of Death:	Castle Hospital, Edinburgh
Parents:	John and Sarah Emma Holloway (nee Briggs)
Address:	Far Cotton, Northampton
Grave Ref:	17275

Additional Information:

Ronald joined the RAF in December 1939. He worked from the age of 15 as a cellar man at the Bridge Street branch of Abington Brewery Co. Ronald was a King's Scout with St Mary's Far Cotton Rover Scout Troop and a member of the Auxiliary Fire Service [AFS]. At his funeral members of the AFS were the guard of honour and Rover Scouts were bearers.

Ronald was the first person to be interred in the area at Towcester Road set aside for Second World War casualties.

Family:

Marriage records, in the December quarter of 1907, show John Holloway married Sarah Emma Briggs, in the district of Hardingstone.

Ronald had a sister Gertrude Mary (born 1911).

James Clinton HOLLWAY
(Name spelt in some records as Holloway and Holling, but spelt Hollway in his own signature to 1911 Census)

Nationality:	British
Rank:	Lieutenant Colonel (Staff Officer)
Regiment:	Royal Defence Corps
Unit:	Commands and Staff
Formerly:	Indian Army and Lincolnshire Regiment
Age at Death:	58
Date of Death:	11th January 1917
Place of Death:	Northampton
Parents:	Major James Hollway and Ida Hollway of Stanhoe Hall, Stanhoe, Norfolk
Wife:	Caroline Jane Hollway (nee Roe)
Address:	31 Worthing Road, Southsea (at time of death)
Grave Ref:	465.1.18038
Medals/Awards:	Mentioned in Despatches

Additional Information:

In 1861 James was living at The Grange, Docking Road, Stanhoe, with his parents, older brother and three servants. His father was described as a Fundholder and County Magistrate. James's father founded the Norfolk Volunteers in 1862. By 1871, one more brother and two sisters had been born and the father was away in the army. James was a pupil at Village Mansion House, Little Wymondley, Herts.

James joined the army in 1879. In 1881 James was serving as a Lieutenant in the 2/17th Foot at Chatham Barracks. James served in the Burma campaign (2 clasps) 1886-7 and 1887-9, Tirah Expedition (2 clasps) 1897-8, (Mentioned in Despatches) and Punjab Frontier 1897-8. James retired from the 128th (Indian) Pioneers with the rank of Lt. Colonel.

In 1911 James was living at 22 Shaftesbury Road, Southsea, with his wife of 29 years, Caroline Jane, his widowed daughter, Ida Caroline Hughes, grandson, Hampden Hughes, and three servants. He had apparently moved to Southsea so that he could enjoy his hobby of yachting. He was Chief Commissioner of the Boy Scout Movement in Portsmouth.

On the outbreak of war he had re-joined and after time in Reading and Nottingham was posted to Northampton. He was responsible, with Lieutenant Colonel Viscount Hood, for drawing up a guard scheme for the railways.

The Northampton Daily Echo reported that "The funeral of Lt. Col. Holloway, who was billeted in Northampton with the Training Reserve, took place with military honours. Fellow officers, detachments from the Training Reserve and Royal Defence Corps provided an escort to the coffin."

Another newspaper reported that he had "suffered a seizure while travelling by train from London and on arriving at Northampton was conveyed in the motor ambulance to the Grand Hotel, where he had been staying for the past three months. Everything was done for the gallant officer, but he never rallied and passed away in the arms of his wife".

James's probate record stated that he died at the Grand Hotel, Northampton. Probate was granted to his wife Caroline and his estate was worth £713 17s 3d (£713.86).

Family:

James married Caroline Jane Roe at Portsea in the June quarter 1881. Their first daughter Ida Caroline was born in Norfolk in 1882 and they must have left for India shortly after. Three more daughters were born, Katherine Clara (1883), Marian Blanche Florence (1886) and Nora May (1888) all in India. Nora May did not live long and died in 1888.

James stayed in India for a considerable time as Ida married in 1903 in India, as did Katherine and Marian in 1905.

James was survived by his widow, three daughters, five grandsons and four granddaughters.

Funeral of James Hollway

William James HOLMES

Nationality:	British
Rank:	Corporal
Service No:	7606
Regiment:	King's Royal Rifle Corps
Unit:	2nd Battalion
Age at Death:	29
Date of Death:	25th October 1918
Place of Death:	Northampton
Parents:	Thomas and Minnie Ann Holmes (nee Smith)
Address:	48 Overstone Road, Northampton (attestation papers)
Wife:	Florence Louise Holmes (nee Wanstall)
Grave Ref:	463.1.17970
Medals/Awards:	1914/15 Star, British, Victory and Silver War Badge

Additional Information:

William was born around 1889 at Ravensthorpe. In 1891, he lived with his parents and younger sister, Beatrice, in Kingsthorpe. In 1901 William lived with his parents at 34 Church Street, Northampton and his father was working as a bank messenger. By the time of his son's death Thomas had become a bank caretaker.

William joined the King's Royal Rifles on 5th November 1906 and gave his occupation as an upholsterer. He was posted to India, via Malta, in January 1909. He returned from India in February 1910. He joined the Army Reserve in November 1913 and re-enlisted on 5th August 1914. He joined the British Expeditionary Force on 26th August 1914 with the 2nd Battalion King's Royal Rifle Corps and was appointed Lance Corporal, unpaid, on 15th March 1915.

He suffered shrapnel wounds to his left elbow on 8th May 1915 and was sent to the Australian Volunteer Hospital and from there back to England on 11th May 1915.

He returned to the Battalion Depot on 12th August 1915 and was posted back to France on 3rd May 1916. He joined his Battalion in the field on

24th May 1916 and was promoted to Corporal the next day. He was wounded but remained at duty. In June at Vimy Ridge he was again wounded, with a gunshot wound to the left leg and side and was sent, via 6th Field Ambulance, to 6th Casualty Clearing Station. He was moved to General Hospital, Camiers and returned home on 10th August 1916 on H.S. Brighton.

The wound caused a fracture of the femur, displaced the knee cap and fractured the head of his tibia. He had to have eight operations on his leg, six of which were carried out in France. He was discharged from Tooting Military Hospital on 25th April 1917 as unfit owing to a stiff knee and still requiring outpatient treatment. He said he was going to live at Bank House, 6 The Parade, Northampton. His character was said to be steady, honest and an excellent NCO [Non Commissioned Officer]. He was issued Silver War Badge No. 260242.

William had married Florence on 13th September 1913 in Elham, Kent. No children are recorded.

William died at home of influenza.

Family:

The 1911 Census showed that William had four siblings, Beatrice (1890); Harry (1894); Christopher (1898); and Stanley (1905). One sibling had died prior to the 1911 Census.

There was a marriage of a Harry Thomas Holmes to an Elsie Smith in 1914. The Commonwealth War Graves site records the death of a Corporal Harry Thomas Holmes, No.13938 of the 6th Battalion of the Northamptonshire Regiment and husband of Elsie on 3rd May 1917. He was commemorated on the Arras Memorial.

Phillip Robert Hector INNS

Nationality:	British
Rank:	Private
Service No:	31790
Regiment:	East Surrey Regiment
Unit:	3rd Battalion
Age at Death:	17
Date of Death:	1st April 1918
Place of Death:	Daventry Registration District
Parents:	John and Ada Elizabeth Inns (nee York)
Address:	93 Cemetery Road, Northampton
Grave Ref:	447.4.17373

Additional Information:

Phillip was born in early 1901, and was on the 1901 Census at St Pauls, Northampton with his parents. They lived at 45 Semilong, Northampton. In 1911 he was still with his parents but they had moved to 93 Semilong. His father was a shoe finisher. John and Ada had been married 32 years.

Phillip enlisted in Northampton. The 3rd (Reserve) Battalion, East Surrey Regiment was a depot training unit throughout the war.

Family:

By the 1911 Census John and Ada had had sixteen children of which only six were alive. We have managed to trace Frances (who died in 1881), Annie (who married a William Collyer in 1897), Florence, Edith Mary, John George, Rosa, Benjamin (who died in 1891), Ida (born 1892 and died in 1896), Frank Thomas (born and died in 1898) and Philip.

John George served as Gunner No. 106447, B Battery, 50th Brigade, Royal Field Artillery. He died on 28th March 1918 and was buried at Toutencourt Communal Cemetery in France.

Henry JENNER

Nationality:	British
Rank:	Driver
Service No:	TS/1175
Regiment:	Army Service Corps
Unit:	1st Horse Transport Company
Age at Death:	53
Date of Death:	15th January 1917
Place of Death:	Northampton General Hospital
Parents:	William and Ann Jenner (nee Mobsby)
Wife:	Mary Ann Emma Jenner (nee Wells)
Address:	Kensington House, Kensington Court, High Street, Kensington, London
Grave Ref:	448.4.17397
Medals/Awards:	1915 Star, Victory and British

Additional Information:

Henry first served with the 4th Dragoon Guards from 3rd March 1885 to 2nd March 1897. Before enlisting he had been a member of the 1st Sussex Artillery Volunteers.

Henry married Mary Ann on 3rd April 1892 and on the 1911 Census they were living at Wargrave Stables, Crawley Ridge, Camberley and he worked as a groom.

He re-enlisted on 19th August 1914, as a batman. He went to France on 16th August 1915, landing in Boulogne and was invalided back to England on 9th November 1916 with pleurisy. There is a note in his record from Brig. Gen. Edward Bailey Ashmore, asking that he be returned to France when he was well as he carried out his duties in an exemplary fashion. Major General Ashmore had a distinguished career ending as one of the original commanders of the Royal Flying Corps during the First World War.

Henry died in Northampton General Hospital from a malignant growth on the right lung. The service was conducted by F. Keysell, vicar of St. Sepulchre's Church. The gun carriage was loaned from Weedon and the escort and firing party came from Northampton Depot.

His widow Mary was given a pension of 15s (£0.75) a week.

Family:

On the 1871 census his father was a labourer in a coal yard and Henry had six siblings, Emily, William, Ann, Caroline, Hannah and Elizabeth.

St Sepulchre's Church, Northampton
Regimental Church for the Northamptonshire Regiment

Courtesy of Dave Humphreys

Thomas JOHNSON

Nationality:	British
Rank:	Private
Service No:	G/669
Regiment:	Middlesex Regiment
Unit:	18th Battalion
Age at Death:	49 (on death registration)
Date of Death:	31st January 1916
Place of Death:	Northampton
Parents:	James and Mary Johnson
Address:	Council Huts, Waterworks, Mardy, Glamorgan
Grave Ref:	448.3.17412
Medals/Awards:	Victory and British

Additional Information:

Thomas Johnson was shown on the 1891 Census as aged 19, living with his parents, and born in Walsall, Staffs. On his attestation papers he gave his age as 43 years and 4 months which would have made his age at death 44. A birth registration for the December quarter of 1870 matches Thomas and, therefore, his actual age at death was most probably 46.

His enlistment papers showed that he had served prior to 1915, with the South Staffordshire Regiment, but no details have been found. He signed up in March 1915, at Hornsey, and joined the Middlesex Regiment, even though he was listed as living in Mardy, Glamorgan at the time.

It is unclear where he served. He died in a fire at the Men's Mess in Abbey Road, Northampton. Articles in the Mercury and Northampton Daily Echo reported that the fire was discovered by PC Enderby of Northampton Borough Police at 12.40 am. It was at the St Mary's Parish Rooms, Abbey Road, Far Cotton. This building had been in military occupation most of the time since the start of the war and was being used by the Middlesex Regiment as a Mess Room. A military fire call was sounded and men billeted in streets nearby rendered valuable assistance. Unfortunately the blaze was too strong and although a person was possibly in the building they were unable to save him and the building was gutted.

Charred remains were discovered and identified as those of Private Thomas Johnson who was a cook for the orderly room staff and the detention prison. He was not supposed to sleep in the building but for some reason (apparently he had said the people at his billet were too religious) had not slept at his billet for some nights. He was an old soldier who had served in South Africa. He had joined 18th Middlesex Public Works Pioneers (navvies) Battalion at Hornsey.

An inquest was held and an accidental death verdict was given. At his funeral the 25th Battalion Middlesex were on parade together with their bugle and drum band. This band, together with the pipes and drums of 24th Battalion Middlesex, led the procession. The coffin was carried by six cooks and placed on a gun carriage and, with a firing party with reversed arms, taken to St Mary's Church for the service. Mrs Mary A Lloyd of Walsall, his sister, attended.

Family:

He was unmarried and his next of kin appeared to be his sister. We can only trace five siblings, Daniel, Annie, Margaret, James and Mary to whom his medals were sent.

FE2B Biplane with the propeller behind the pilot's cockpit. This is the type of plane whose propeller struck William Joseph Kelly causing his death.

(see page 121)

Arthur JONES

Nationality: British
Rank: Lance Corporal
Service No: 5881020
Regiment: Grenadier Guards
Unit: Foot Guards
Age at Death: 29
Date of Death: 1st June 1940
Place of Death: Northampton
Parents: Harry and Nellie Jones (later Freeman)
(Stepfather Mr E E Freeman)
Address: 150 Euston Road, Northampton
Grave Ref: Grave 17276
Medals/Awards: 1939-45 War Medal 1939-1945 Star

Additional Information:

Arthur was a Reservist recalled at the outbreak of the Second World War and went to France with the Grenadier Guards as a Lance Corporal. He died in hospital of wounds received in action with the British Expeditionary Force.

Prior to his recall he worked as a meter reader and collector for Northampton Electric Light and Power Co.

Family:

The 1911 census record showed he was seven months old, lived in Inkerman Terrace and he was the son of Harry Jones who was also buried in Towcester Road Cemetery and died in the First World War (see next page).

Harry JONES

Nationality:	British
Rank:	Private
Service No:	42918
Regiment:	Manchester Regiment
Unit:	2/5th Battalion
Age at Death:	37
Date of Death:	31st August 1917
Place of Death:	Home
Wife:	Nellie Jones (later Freeman)
Address:	8 Inkerman Terrace, Northampton
Grave Ref:	465.1.18026
Medals/Awards:	Victory and British

Additional Information:

Harry had a previous service number, 45067, Bedfordshire Regiment. His service record could not be found.

The Northampton Daily Echo reported "Harry Jones of the Manchester Regiment died at 4th London General Hospital, Denmark Hill. He was given a funeral with full military honours with a service at St Sephulchre's Church followed by internment at Towcester Road. The Training Reserve provided bearers, firing party and bugler. His wife living at 8 Inkerman Terrace attended the funeral together with his brothers Thomas, James, Bert, William, Private Jesse and their wives, Mr & Mrs Newton, father and mother in law, and others. A wreath was sent from Padmore & Barnes." It is assumed he had worked at this firm.

Family:

According to the 1911 census, he was living at the above address with his wife Nellie and their two children Emily (3) and Arthur (7 months), and worked as a shoe finisher.

His son Arthur died of wounds in action in 1940, and was also buried in Towcester Road Cemetery (see previous page).

William Joseph KELLY

Nationality:	Canadian
Rank:	Lieutenant
Regiment:	Royal Air Force
Unit:	Royal Navy Air Service
Age at Death:	21
Date of Death:	26th September 1918
Parents:	Patrick R. and Elizabeth Jordon Kelly (nee Fitzpatrick)
Address:	49 Nelson Street, Brantford, Ontario, Canada
Grave Ref:	463,1,17974
Medals/Awards:	Victory and British

Additional Information:

William attested on 6th February 1917 in Toronto Canada where he was living and worked as a banker. He stated that he was born on 6th April 1897, in Brantford, Ontario and his mother, Elizabeth, was his next of kin living at the address given above.

The Forces War Records site lists his rank as a Probationary Flight Officer in the Royal Navy Air Service. He was at the No. 1 School of Navigation & Bomb Dropping (Pilot) and was accidentally killed when struck by a propeller of FE2b No.B1856 (see picture of the plane on page 118).

There is a death registration for Brixworth District for a William J Kelly aged 23. This is the closest match to the date and age given for William.

No. 1 School of Navigation and Bomb Dropping was based near Stonehenge.

Additional Sources: Forces War Records

Charles Robert KENDALL

Nationality: British
Rank: Staff Serjeant
Service No: 03268
Regiment: Royal Army Ordnance Corps
Unit: 66th (S) Company
Age at Death: 51
Date of Death: 5th March 1917
Place of Death: Northampton
Parents: William and Kate Kendall
Wife: Mary Kendall (nee Watts)
Address: 128 Kingsley Park Terrace, Northampton
Grave Ref: 448.4.17393
Medals/Awards: Victory and British

Additional Information:

Born in Paulerspury on 23rd February 1865, Charles was the eldest of 14 children.

He enlisted on the 3rd January 1885 at Stamford aged 19 (a carpenter) in the Lincolnshire Regiment as Private No. 985. He joined the regiment in India in September 1885 and was made Lance Corporal in July 1886 and further promoted Corporal in 1888. On 15th September 1892 he transferred to King's Own Yorkshire Light Infantry as Private No. 4608 and was posted to the Ordnance Depot.

In December 1898 Charles was transferred to the 2nd Border Regiment and back to the 1st Battalion Lincolnshire Regiment, Indian Ordnance Department in 1904. He remained with the battalion until being discharged on 13th April 1907 as Serjeant No. 7339. He served over 21 years in the army, nearly all in India, gaining the Long Service and Good Conduct Medal and his character was described as exemplary.

He was listed as a soldier on the 1901 census. He lived with his parents and was a widower. He was home from India on sick leave. There were three grandchildren, Herbert 9, Percy 7 and Bessie 6 at the same address (see Family).

Charles re-enlisted on 21st December 1914 at Woolwich as a Private No. 03268 in the Army Ordnance Corps and two days later was promoted Staff Serjeant. He was posted to France on 21st July 1915. On 25th October 1915 he was admitted to the 15th Casualty Clearing Station and later taken to 3rd Canadian General Hospital and finally transferred to England on 14th November 1915.

He was in Preston Hospital with colic from 17th July to 1st September 1916 and then sent back to duty. Two weeks later he was admitted to the Military Hospital Northampton with chronic laryngitis and was transferred the same day to Duston Military Hospital (Berrywood).

On 1st December 1916 he was again transferred, this time to Abington Avenue, VAD Auxiliary Hospital with tubercular laryngitis. He was back at Duston in early 1917 and was discharged on 2nd March 1917 at Burscough, Lancashire due to sickness. He was given a Silver War Badge No. 140805. He died three days later at home aged 51.

On his discharge papers he stated that he had served as a Temporary Warder in HM Prisons and a Special Constable, County and Borough Police Force.

Family:

The grandchildren on the 1901 Census were born to Robert Charles Kendal and Annie Helena Maud Kendall. Herbert was born in Cawnpore, Bengal and Percy and Bessie in Poona, Bombay. There was a marriage between Charles and Annie on 14th May 1890 in Cawnpore, India.

Herbert, the son of Charles, was serving with the 2nd Northamptonshire Regiment in Malta at the time of the 1911 Census. He had enlisted in about 1908. He would have gone with the 2nd Battalion to Egypt in January 1914. When war broke out the 2nd was recalled from Egypt and went to France on 6th November 1914. Herbert went with them as a Corporal in A Company. He wrote a letter to the Independent in January 1915 thanking them for gifts. He was promoted to Lance Serjeant No. 8777.

Herbert died on 14th March 1915 aged 23. This was the last day of the battle of Neuve Chapelle where the 2nd Battalion was practically wiped out. From a total of 19 officers and about 600 other ranks at the start there were 17 officer casualties of which nine were killed. Casualties for other ranks numbered 414 of which 102 were killed, 83 missing and 203 wounded. The missing were almost all later assumed dead. Herbert is commemorated on the Le Touret Memorial in France. There are 13,455 war graves in this cemetery.

We have been unable to find Percy on the 1911 Census. Bessie was at the Albion Hill House, Finsbury Road, Brighton which appears to be a school for girls.

There was a fourth child from this marriage, Charles Benjamin, who was born in 1896 in Bombay and died in 1899.

Annie died in 1900 in India.

Herbert married for the second time to Mary on 4th March 1902 and had one child, Charles Robert, born in July 1906 in Wembley, Middlesex.

Funeral of an Old "Steelback."

Photo: C. R. Rathbone.

Funeral of Francis William Land (see page 126)

124

Herbert Victor KENNEDY

Nationality:	British (born near Dublin)
Rank:	Serjeant
Service No:	29604
Regiment:	Royal Field Artillery
Unit:	"A" Instructional Battery
Age at Death:	34
Date of Death:	7th November 1918
Place of Death:	Northampton
Parents:	George
Address:	32 Military Road, Northampton.
Grave Ref:	446.2.17319
Medals/Awards:	1914 Star, Victory and British, South Africa and the Silver War Badge

Additional Information:

Victor was originally in the militia (3rd Northamptonshire Regiment). In January 1903, when he was 18 and a baker by trade, he joined the Royal Field Artillery. Victor served in South Africa (1905-06), in India (1906-14) and at the start of the First World War went to France (1914-17).

He was taken ill in 1916 in France and returned to the UK. He was discharged on 11th May 1917 and spent his last days in a Northampton sanatorium.

Family:

Father George (32 Military Road, Northampton), brother Howard (34 Alfred Street, Northampton) and sister Mabel Tibbett (18 Austin Street, Northampton).

Francis William LAND

Nationality:	British
Rank:	Company Serjeant Major
Service No:	5006
Regiment:	Northamptonshire Regiment
Unit:	2nd Battalion
Age at Death:	43
Date of Death:	8th May 1921
Place of Death:	Northampton
Parents:	Francis David and Elizabeth Land (nee Harrison)
Wife:	Alice Sarah Land (nee Hayes)
Address:	47 Earl Street, Northampton
Grave Ref:	445.3.17292
Medals/Awards:	Distinguished Conduct Medal. 1914 Star, British and Victory plus Queens South African Medal with 3 clasps, Belmont, Orange Free State and Transvaal. Kings South African Medal with 2 clasps 1901 and 1902

Additional Information:

Francis was born in Norwich on 22nd September 1878. The 1891 Census showed he lived with his parents in Norwich. His father was an engine fitter and Francis a mustard packer.

He became a career soldier who joined the Northamptonshire Regiment in 1896 having already served in the 4th Battalion of the Norfolk Regiment. Francis served in South Africa from October 1899 to May 1904; India, January 1908 to March 1911 and, Malta, March 1911 to January 1914.

The 1911 Census recorded him as 32, Serjeant, married, serving in the 2nd Northamptonshire Regiment in Malta. He then moved to Egypt where he stayed until October 1914 and moved to France on 6th November 1914. He served with distinction throughout the First World War winning the Distinguished Conduct Medal. The citation reads:

"For conspicuous gallantry at Neuve Chapelle on 13th March 1915, when he took command of the company after his officer had fallen, and handled the men with much ability against a very heavy counter-attack by the enemy."

He was wounded on 18th May 1915 with gunshot wounds to the forehead and leg and was moved to England, on 24th May, for recovery. He was discharged on 14th March 1919 but he re-joined the army in April 1921 and was promoted to Regimental Serjeant Major. He died in Northampton General Hospital a month later (8th May 1921) from pneumonia.

A report in the Independent stated ".....Serjeant Major Land, of 47 Earl Street, Northampton, a well-known ex-warrant officer of the Northamptonshire Regiment died in Northampton Hospital on Sunday. Deceased, who had many years' service to his credit in various battalions of the Northampton's, went to France early in the war and was wounded and eventually invalided out of the service. He volunteered for service in the force raised in consequence of industrial unrest and this act undoubtedly aggravated his ill health and hastened the end."

A photograph of Francis's funeral is on page 124.

The industrial unrest in 1921 was a miners strike which was not originally supported by other workers but led to the General Strike in 1926.

Family:

Francis had six siblings, Rosa, Thomas, Herbert, May, John and David all of whom appear to have survived the war.

Francis and Alice had five children, Alice (born 1908 in Poona, India), Doris (1911 Malta), Phyllis (1912 Malta), Frances (1916 Thrussington) and William (1920 Northampton).

Frederick Thomas Debron LAPWORTH

Nationality:	British
Rank:	Private
Regiment:	Northamptonshire Regiment (Service Nos. 23960 and 4741)
Transferred to:	Royal Defence Corps (No. 28298)
Unit:	65th Company
Age at Death:	49 (Death Registration) 40 on CWGC
Date of Death:	7th February 1917
Place of Death:	Northampton
Parents:	Robert and Louisa C Lapworth (nee Debron)
Wife:	Mary Ann Lapworth (nee Walton)
Address:	(His) 9 Fort St., Northampton
Grave Ref:	465.1.18034
Medals/Awards:	Victory and British plus the South Africa medal with Cape Colony and Transvaal clasps

Additional Information:

Frederick was born about 1868, in St Clements in Oxford where his father worked as a college servant.

He joined the Dorsetshire Regiment in 1884 stating he was 18, but had already been in the Berkshire Militia and was using the name Frederick Oakley. He served in the Mediterranean and Egypt, returned home and then went to Malta and Egypt again. He was again returned home and then was sent to South Africa. He was discharged after returning from South Africa but enlisted for the militia between 1903 and 1907.

On his attestation papers he stated that he worked for the London and North Western Railway in Northampton and that he was born in Woodstock, Oxfordshire.

It was reported that he died at Duston War Hospital.

Family:

Frederick and Mary stated they had six children, however, only five are shown on the 1911 Census; Frederick, Winifred, Olive, Arthur and Rhoda. Another son, Percival, was mentioned on his service record which started in 1903. A daughter Muriel was born later in 1911.

Frederick had nine siblings, Robert, Henry, William, John (also appears to have been a professional soldier), Cecil, Louis, Louisa, Herbert and Kate.

Two brothers also served in WW1.

John was a trooper in the 2nd Life Guards from 1890 to 1909. He was called-up into the RAF in August 1918 and served until March 1919.

Cecil joined the 1st Royal Berkshire Regiment in 1890 rising to the rank of Quarter-Master Serjeant. He went to France from 12th August to 13th November 1914 and was discharged on 7th September 1915.

This inscription commemorates the death of Mary Ann in 1940. It is on the reverse of Frederick's headstone

Peter Walter LATHAM

Nationality:	British
Rank:	Private
Service No:	12655
Regiment:	Norfolk Regiment
Unit:	7th Battalion, A Company
Age at Death:	20
Date of Death:	23rd January 1916
Place of Death:	Northampton
Parents:	Peter and Annie Sarah Carpenter Whetham Latham
Address:	21 Colet Gardens, West Kensington.
Grave Ref:	448.2.17411
Medals/Awards:	1915 Star, Victory and British

Additional Information:

Peter was born in 1895 in the Fulham Registration District. In 1901 he lived with his parents. His father was a tennis and racquet professional instructor, of 18 Elm Gardens, Hammersmith. The 1911 Census showed the family was living in Colet Gardens, West Kensington but Peter was away at school in Margate.

He probably enlisted at St. Paul's Churchyard, in Middlesex and arrived in France on 30th May 1915. He was returned to the General Hospital in Northampton by convoy on 6th January 1916. He was suffering from a scalp wound and a bullet in the brain.

Family:

According to the 1911 Census Peter was one of five children of which three were still living. Those found are Percy (born 1890 and died 1892); Emily Gustave who was still alive in 1930, and Hilda who died in 1993.

Edwin James LEE

Nationality:	British
Rank:	Private
Service No:	10089
Regiment:	Northamptonshire Regiment
Unit:	5th Battalion
Age at Death:	26
Date of Death:	2nd October 1918
Place of Death:	Halifax Registration District
Grave Ref:	446.3.17332
Medals/Awards:	1915 Star, Victory and British

Additional Information:

Edwin's service number was issued in August 1914. He went to France on 31st May 1915 with the 5th Battalion. The Battalion was trained as a fighting battalion, then became a Pioneer Battalion and carried out road and trench repairs near to the front line.

The dataset 'Soldiers who Died in the Great War' stated that Edwin was born in Northampton. The only person who fits this is an Edwin James Lee born in 1891 in Northampton who appears to have swapped his first names on various documents. On the 1901 Census he was listed as James Lee living with his grandmother. His two siblings were living with his father Edwin Lee. By the time of the 1911 Census James was living with his uncle, grandmother and his two siblings. This gave his age as 19. These details tie in with a recorded death of a James E Lee in Halifax aged 26 in the December quarter of 1918.

Family:

Edwin had two younger brothers, William Owen and Cecil Wadsworth who appear to have survived the war.

Thomas LEWIS

Nationality:	British
Rank:	Private
Service No:	23207
Regiment:	Royal Defence Corps
Unit:	66th Company
Date of Death:	24th November 1918
Grave Ref:	446.4.17313
Medals/Awards:	Victory and British

Additional Information:

There is a Death Registration for a Thomas Lewis in Northampton aged 53 which might be a match. Thomas's burial record shows that he died at the Northants War Hospital, Upton. His address was unknown.

We have been unable to verify any further information about Thomas.

Employees of Oceanic Works, St James, present ambulance to the Voluntary Aid Detachment

William Edward LUCAS

Nationality:	British
Rank:	Private
Service No:	3/9926
Regiment:	Northamptonshire Regiment
Unit:	2nd Battalion (Depot)
Age at Death:	24
Date of Death:	30th June 1918
Place of Death:	Shoreham Hospital
Parents:	Edwin and Eliza Lucas (nee Law)
Grave Ref:	464.1.18010
Medals/Awards:	1914 Star with clasp, Victory and British

Additional Information:

William was born in St Edmund's parish. On the 1901 Census William lived with his father and two siblings. His father was shown as a widower. The 1911 Census showed that William was living with his father and worked as a General Labourer with the Corporation.

It appears that he joined the regiment in 1914, before the outbreak of war, and would have received basic training at the Depot in Barrack Road. He was probably in England when war broke out, and then drafted to the 2nd Battalion in October 1914.

William travelled to France from Southampton, disembarking at Le Havre on 6th November 1914. William was wounded sometime between the 10th and 14th March 1915, at Neuve Chapelle, when he received a gunshot wound to his thigh, and was returned to England on 20th March 1915.

On his recovery William was sent back to the 2nd Battalion in France. In August 1916 William was again wounded, most likely when the Battalion was heavily engaged near High Wood from 14th to 21st August. The Battalion suffered 373 casualties of which 61 were killed, 252 wounded and 60 missing.

The Northampton Daily Chronicle reported that the Voluntary Aid Detachment arranged return of his body to Northampton and that he had a brother Thomas J who served in the 1/4th Northamptonshire Regiment. This is almost certainly the John shown on the 1911 Census.

Family:

William had two siblings, Minnie and John.

As stated above John served with the 1/4th Northamptonshire Regiment as Private, No. 200395 from 9 September 1914 to 14th April 1917. He was discharged sick and awarded a Silver War Badge.

1914 Star with Clasp

The ribbon is, from left to right, red white and blue

(For further information see Campaign Medals and Awards on page 221)

Thomas LUCK

Nationality: British
Rank: Private
Service No: 23791 (Northampton Regiment)
36089 (Machine Gun Corps)
WR/347494 (Royal Engineers)
Regiment: Grave shows Royal Engineers
Age at Death: 49
Date of Death: 26th May 1922
Place of Death: Northampton
Parents: William E and Ann Luck
Grave Ref: 462.17289
Medals/Awards: Victory and British

Additional Information:

Thomas's father, William, was born about 1836 and Ann, his mother, about 1838 and on the 1871 Census they lived at 33 Birds Piece in St Edmund's parish with their other children. William worked as a shoe riveter.

On the 1881 Census the family consisted of his mother Ann together with Thomas aged 8; his brother Albert, and his sister Ann. They were living at 13 Pike Lane together with 2 lodgers. Ann was shown as a widow, doing washing, and Albert aged 19 was a labourer.

In 1891 Thomas and his mother, Ann, were living at 8 Clark's Yard, Northampton. Thomas, 18, was a coalman and Ann was still doing washing.

No record can be found on the 1901 Census for Thomas.

By 1911, aged 38, Thomas was still in the coal trade and a lodger at 8 Castle Street, a Lodging House. There were 100 people living in the house on the night of the census. His mother died in 1913.

Because of his age Thomas was unlikely to have been called up before 1916. It appears he was trained first in the Northampton Regiment, transferring to the Machine Gun Corps (this certainly would have not been before 1916 as MGC were not formed until about this time and his number was not an early one). Finally he was posted to the Royal Engineers and this would have been after 1st January 1917. The WR prefix to this registration number indicates he was in the Transport Branch of the Royal Engineers.

It is assumed he was demobilised as he would have been given a new number if he stayed in after 1920.

Family:

Thomas may have had six siblings, two brothers, Albert and George and four sisters, Kate, Emma, Fanny and Ann. Albert and George appear to have survived the war.

Richard Galley Collection

Courtesy of Richard Galley

Highland Division based in Bedford

William MARRIOTT

Nationality:	British
Rank:	Lance Serjeant
Service No:	TT/03131
Regiment:	Royal Army Veterinary Corps [RAVC]
Unit:	Highland Division Veterinary Hospital
Age at Death:	46
Date of Death:	30th December 1916
Place of Death:	Aylesbury Registration District
Wife:	Emma Marriott (nee Caiger)
Grave Ref:	137.4.5338

Additional Information:

William enlisted at Bedford into the RAVC, attached to the Highland Division Veterinary Hospital. The Corps was responsible for the medical care of animals used by the army, mainly horses, mules and pigeons.

One of the reasons that he joined at Bedford may be due to the fact that the Highland Division had moved south at the outbreak of the war and was concentrated in the area of Bedford.

Ordered to prepare for France, on 13th April 1915 the Division moved via Southampton and Folkestone and was in France by 5th May. On 11th May 1915, 1/1st Highland Division was renamed 51st Highland Division.

William died at Aylesbury VAD Hospital. His funeral started from 14 Shakespeare Road, Northampton, where his widow was living. The Royal Field Artillery provided a gun carriage; and the Depot a bugler and firing party. Lance Serjeants from the RAVC carried his coffin. His brother H T Marriott attended. He was the proprietor of the County Hotel, Abington.

William was buried in a family grave just outside the war graves section at Towcester Road.

Family:

The 1911 Census showed William married to Emma, with a daughter Florrie. Also living at the same address was an Edward Caiger. Marriage traced of a William Marriott to an Emily Florence Caiger in December quarter 1901 and a daughter Florence Beatrice born in 1902. It is likely that Edward Caiger was Emily's father.

Courtesy of Richard Galley

The Highland Divisions based in Bedford

John Arthur MAXWELL

Nationality:	Australian
Rank:	Private
Service No:	926
Regiment:	Australian Infantry (AIF)
Unit:	26th Battalion, 7th Infantry Brigade
Age at Death:	36 (gave age at enlistment as 34½ but Death Registration gives his age as 34)
Date of Death:	10th September 1916
Place of Death:	Northampton
Grave Ref:	448.4.17401
Medals/Awards:	1915 Star, Victory and British

Additional Information:

John was born in Glenorchy, Tasmania and in 1914 worked as a labourer, living at Burnie on the north coast of Tasmania. On 24th February 1915 he enlisted at Ulverstone about 40 km along the coast from Burnie. His brother William Alexander, also of Burnie, was named as next of kin. He had a sister, Agnes Virginia, from whom he had not heard for many years.

John embarked from Brisbane on 29th June 1915 and, after training in Egypt, the Battalion left Alexandria for Gallipoli on 4th September 1915. It landed there on 12th September, playing a purely defensive role. It withdrew from the peninsula on 12th December and returned to Alexandria from Mudros on 9th January 1916.

John left Alexandria on 15th March 1916 for the Western Front and landed at Marseilles on 21st March 1916. The Battalion fought in its first major battle around Pozières between 28th July and 7th August 1916.

On 26th August 1916, John received gunshot wounds to the back and was taken to No.3 Casualty Clearing Station in France. He was quickly transferred by train to No. 3 Canadian General Hospital at Boulogne. He was moved on quickly by hospital ship to Newhaven, England. On 2nd September, seriously ill, John arrived at Northampton War Hospital Duston, where he died.

Family:

John's brother, William, was living in Branxholm, Tasmania in July 1917 and appears to have died before 1920. His sister Agnes was married and lived in Spotswood, Australia in 1920.

Sydney Donaldson, from Australia, grandson of Charles McGoldrick, laying wreath at the ANZAC Day Ceremony 2013.

See page 143

Courtesy of Geoff Grainger

WILLIAM McCANN

Nationality:	British
Rank:	Regimental Serjeant Major [RSM]
Service No:	36706
Regiment:	Lincolnshire Regiment
Formerly:	Lancashire Fusiliers
Age at Death:	54
Date of Death:	25th April 1917
Place of Death:	Northampton Registration District
Parents:	John and Una McCann
Wife:	Martha Elizabeth McCann
Address:	35 St James Square, Holland Park, London
Grave Ref:	448.3.17388
Medals/Awards:	Victory and British

Additional Information:

William's father, John, came from Ireland and was serving in Malta in 1865 with the 100th Regiment (Prince of Wales Royal Canadian), where William's older sister was born. John left Malta with the Regiment to return to England in 1867 and it appears William was born at sea on the journey.

Aged 4 in 1871, he lived in the Wellington Barracks in Bolton Road, Bury, Lancashire with his father, aged 34, by now a Serjeant Major; and his mother Una, aged 27, born in Essex; and his sister.

It has not been possible to identify William on the 1881 Census.

By 1891 William was married to Martha and served as a Colour Serjeant with the 20th Regiment, Lancashire Fusiliers, again at Wellington Barracks. He may have been involved in training the militia. On the Census he stated that he was born in Wigan and his wife gave Ireland as her place of birth.

Ten years later, in the 1901 Census, he had become a Quartermaster Serjeant, and had two daughters, Ida aged 5, and Amy 2. He was stationed at Wellington Barracks, his wife Martha then gave Bury as her birth place.

The 1911 Census showed he had left the army with a pension and was living in Heaton Moor, Stockport with his wife and two daughters. He and his wife were steward and stewardess of a club at 38 Shaw Street, and were still there in 1914. Martha gave her birth place as Fermoy, Ireland.

His service number for Lancashire Fusiliers was given as No. 27167 and this is most likely the number given to him when he re-enlisted. Sometime after this he was transferred as RSM No. 36706 to the Lincolnshire Regiment. From his Medal Card he did not go overseas before 1917 and it is most likely he stayed in the UK due to his age. When he died of pneumonia he was attached to the Depot (possibly Sobraon Barracks, Lincoln) and it is assumed he trained recruits.

His headstone has the badge of the Lancashire Regiment but states "Lincolnshire Regiment late of the Lancashire Regiment".

Family:

William and Martha had two children at the time of the 1911 Census, Ida and Amy. One child had died before the Census was taken.

This inscription is on the reverse of William's headstone. It commemorates Martha's death in 1929.

Charles Henry McGOLDRICK

Nationality:	Australian
Rank:	Private
Service No:	5183
Regiment:	Australian Infantry (AIF)
Unit:	16th Reinforcements, 1st Battalion
Age at Death:	25
Date of Death:	16th September 1916
Place of Death:	Northampton
Parents:	Charles M and Mary Louise McGoldrick (nee Head)
Wife:	Sarah Irene McGoldrick of Port Kembla, New South Wales, Australia
Grave Ref:	448.2.17399
Medals/Awards:	Victory and British

Additional Information:

Born in Mount Keira, near Wollongong, New South Wales about 16th October 1890. In 1913 he married Sarah Irene Lindsay at Woonona, New South Wales where he was working as a miner.

143

Charles enlisted in the 16th Reinforcements, 1st Battalion on 14th December 1914 at Stanwell Park, on the coast just north of Wollongong. He was posted to Liverpool, New South Wales. He embarked at Sydney on SS Makarini on 1st April 1916 and disembarked at Suez on 2nd May 1916. Later he sailed on SS Caledonian from Alexandria to Marseilles arriving on 17th May. Charles was sent to Étaples to report to 1st Australian Divisions Depot. The next month he suffered a hernia and was in 26th General Hospital for over a week. Charles returned to the Depot at Étaples on 27th July and joined the 1st Infantry Battalion of the Australian Imperial Force.

On the 18th August 1916 he was severely wounded in the right knee (at this time the 1st Battalion were fighting near Mouquet Farm near Pozières) and was admitted to No. 8 Casualty Clearing Station. He was transferred by No. 31 Ambulance Train to Wimereux on 26th August, Charles was moved on, via Boulogne, to Northampton Hospital on 2nd September 1916. His leg was amputated at the thigh in Northampton Hospital on 9th September which left him seriously ill. Charles was transferred to Duston Hospital where he died of pneumonia on 16th September 1916.

When his wife Sarah was informed of his death she was living in Scarborough, South Coast, New South Wales. A record has been found for a child, called Irene Ada, born in 1913. See photo above taken before he left Australia.

Family:

Two siblings have been found, Selina C (born 1888) and Ester M (1894)

His grandson, Sydney Donaldson, came to the UK in 2013 and laid a wreath at the ANZAC Day Ceremony at Towcester Road Cemetery. See photo page 140.

Ernest MEIN

Nationality:	Canadian
Rank:	Private
Service No:	916147
Regiment:	2nd Canadian Mounted Rifles Battalion
Age at Death:	27
Date of Death:	9th October 1918
Place of Death:	Northampton
Parents:	Robert and Jessie Mein
Address:	538 Harvey Street, Peterborough, Ontario, Canada
Grave Ref:	446.2.17331

Additional Information:

Ernest was born in Peterborough, Ontario, Canada on 9th October 1891. In 1916 he lived at 4 Constance Street, Toronto and worked as a druggist at W R Hoar chemist of Roncesvalles Avenue. He was a member of the Parkdale Presbyterian Church and also Parkdale Canoe Club. Aged 24 years and 4 months he enlisted at Toronto in the 198th (Buffs) Battalion of the Canadian Overseas Expeditionary Force on 28th February 1916.

He went overseas to France and transferred to the 2nd Canadian Mounted Rifles Battalion which had retrained from cavalry to infantry. The Battalion was part of the 8th Canadian Infantry Brigade in the 3rd Canadian Division which fought on the Western Front.

From 26th to 30th August 1918 the 3rd Canadian Division was involved in the Battle of the Scarpe and captured Monchy le Preux during the second battle of Arras. This is most likely where he was wounded on 26th August 1918. He died at Weston Favell Hospital on 9th October 1918.

Family:

A report of Ernest's death in the Toronto Star of 19th October 1918, stated he had a sister, only identified as Mrs W H Lang of Toronto.

Weston Favell St John's Hospital

William MERRIMAN

Nationality:	British
Rank:	Lance Corporal
Service No:	S/31224
Regiment:	Army Service Corps [ASC]
Age at Death:	25
Date of Death:	7th July 1918
Place of Death:	Oswestry Registration District
Parents:	William and Elizabeth Merriman
Grave Ref:	305.3.11868
Medals/Awards:	1914 Star, Victory and British

Additional Information:

William's father, also William, worked as a leather currier and was born in Bristol about 1839. His mother, Elizabeth, was born in Northampton about 10 years later. In 1891 the family were living with their nine children at 44 St Mary Street, Northampton. William, the youngest, was born in 1892. The family had moved to 56b Sheep Street by 1901.

In 1911, William lived with his father and two sisters at 22 Holly Road, Northampton. His mother had died in 1904, aged 55. The Merriman's were sharing the house with another family, probably his married sister Louisa, her husband and their child. William worked as a mercantile clerk.

He appears to have enlisted at Northampton in the ASC at the outbreak of the war, going to France on 21st September 1914. The S in his army number usually denoted the Supply Branch of the ASC, possibly using his clerical skills, although the army was not known for being this logical. If this was the case he would have required little training and this may be why he was in France very quickly or he may have been a part time soldier pre-war.

He was promoted Acting Serjeant by the time he died on 7th July 1918 in England. His father died in 1919, aged 81.

Family:

William's siblings were Frederick William, Joseph Henry, Amelia, Elizabeth, Louisa, Leonard, Thomas, Martha, Frank, Oliver H and Emma.

**William is buried outside the
Commonwealth War Grave Section**

Edward MILLS

Nationality:	British
Rank:	Rifleman
Service No:	206312
Regiment:	Rifle Brigade
Unit:	24th Battalion
Age at Death:	48
Date of Death:	3rd April 1920
Place of Death:	Leicester Registration District
Parents:	Thomas William and Ellen Mills (nee Chambers)
Address:	57 Adelaide Street, Northampton
Grave Ref:	462.1.17938
Medals/Awards:	British

Additional Information:

Edward's first army number was Private No.163 in the Rifle Brigade. Numbers in this range were issued in about 1889 when he was 17. This would have been a regular army unit.

The 24th (Home Counties) Battalion was a Territorial Battalion made up of supernumerary Territorial Companies formed from National Reservists who were used for guarding vulnerable points in Great Britain. In 1916, the 24th went to India to carry out Garrison duty. It appears he was recalled from the National Reserve when the war started and possibly went to India.

The British Medal he was awarded appears to have been returned but there is no explanation in the records. He did not receive the Victory Medal. Qualification for the Victory Medal required mobilisation in any service and entry to a theatre of war between 5th August 1914 and 11th November 1918. Only the frontier regions of India qualified as a theatre of war, so it would seem that Edward did not serve in these areas.

The strongest link we have between Edward and his mother Ellen is that in 1914 he was listed as an Absent Voter at his mother's address of 57 Adelaide Street, Northampton which was the address on the Commonwealth War Graves Commission record.

No Census or birth record can be found for Edward but there is an Edward born c1870 in Malta on the 1911 Census. This Edward is a Serjeant at Sheerness Dockyard.

Family:

Edward's grandparents appear to be James and Hannah Chambers who lived in Northampton; and his parents Thomas William and Ellen Mills. There seems to be three siblings Beatrice E (born 1879), Sidney A (1884) and Grace E (1885), (all dates approximate). Edward's parents do not appear to have lived together until the 1901 Census when they are living in Hardingstone, Northampton and Thomas is shown as ex Royal Marines.

Courtesy of Robert Cutts

Rifle Brigade Memorial, Grosvenor Gardens, London

Charles MOORE

Nationality:	British
Rank:	Private
Service No:	19447
Regiment:	Northamptonshire Regiment
Age at Death:	42
Date of Death:	7th January 1916
Place of Death:	Northampton
Parents:	John and Hanna Moore
Grave Ref:	449.3.17420
Medals/Awards:	1915 Star, Victory and British

Additional Information:

The dataset 'Soldiers who Died in the Great War' gave Charles's birth place as Radford, Nottinghamshire. The only birth at Radford is in 1870 and this ties in with the Moore family living at Mitchell Road, Radford on the 1871 Census. However, if this date of birth is accurate this would make him 46 when he died.

The only record that fits for Charles in the 1881 Census, placed him still in Mitchell Street but his age was two years younger and his mother was three years younger. He did have a sister but her name was Sarah thus unlikely to be the Mrs E Hall who applied for his medals. Unable to find a record for Charles in the 1901 and 1911 Census but he could have been overseas at that time with the army.

Prior to joining the Northamptonshire Regiment, Charles served as a Private with the Sherwood Foresters (Notts and Derby) Regiment with a service number of 6953. This number was issued in about 1901. By 1914 he was most likely to be on the Reserve. He re-enlisted on 11th September 1914 at Derby, into the Sherwood Foresters Regiment.

Charles was drafted to France on 13th July 1915. On 21st July, 99 Other Ranks from the Sherwood Foresters were posted to the 2nd Battalion Northamptonshire Regiment near Sailly. They reinforced the Battalion after it suffered 426 casualties at Aubers Ridge. He was one of those transferred. His number in the Northamptonshire Regiment was in the range given to men transferred from other regiments.

On 4th October 1915, he was admitted to a convalescence hospital at Boulogne. The record showed that he had nephritis and contusion of the mouth. He was discharged but readmitted to 2nd General Hospital, Boulogne and sent back to England on 15th November, to a convalescence hospital at Herne Bay. Later he was given sick leave to 39 Victoria Street, Long Eaton. On 20th December he was sent to Northampton Barracks; declared fit for light duties, and posted to A Company. A medical on 25th December, stated that he was likely to be ready for normal service in six months.

Charles was found dead in bed at the Barracks on the night of 7th January 1916. It was reported in the Northampton Daily Echo that "he had died after going to bed fighting drunk and falling over. The inquest found that he died from a burst blood vessel in the brain thought to have been caused by Moore being in an excited state".

It was reported that his previous occupation was a lace operative and that his mother lived at Burton Joyce, Derby.

Family:

Charles's siblings appeared to be Jane, Sarah, Frank and Hannah.

Herne Bay.—Railwaymen's Convalescent Home, Library

Herne Bay Railwayman's Convalescent Home which was used for soldiers during WW1

Frederick MUSGROVE

Nationality:	British
Rank:	Private
Service No:	25404
Regiment:	Essex Regiment
Age at Death:	44 (Death registration shows 46)
Date of Death:	2nd July 1919
Place of Death:	Northampton
Parents:	Richard Musgrove
Wife:	Phoebe Eliza Musgrove (nee Pitt)
Grave Ref:	445.3.17300
Medals/Awards:	British and Silver War Badge

Additional Information:

Frederick was born in 1875 in Lambeth and his father, Richard, was a pill maker. Frederick married Phoebe Eliza Pitt in 1895 when he was living at 70 Frederick Street, London and Phoebe lived nearby at 58.

Frederick enlisted, aged 40, on 9th June 1915 at Hornsey for band duty in the 25th Reserve Battalion, Middlesex Regiment. At that time he was living at 25 Moneyer Street, London with the trade of clerk and musician. His wife Phoebe and five of their children were at home. Winifred, the youngest, was less than 3 months old.

Formed at Tring in October 1915 from the Depot Companies of 18th, 19th, and 26th Battalions and the 15th Reserve Battalion, the Middlesex Regiment moved to Northampton and in May 1916 to Aldershot. This may be when he became involved with Northampton.

On 28th January 1916 he was transferred as Private No. 25404 to the 2nd Garrison Battalion Essex Regiment. Frederick left England to serve overseas in India on 24th February 1916. On 9th November 1916, after being ill with heart trouble while in India, he was taken by hospital ship from Bombay to 17th General Hospital at Alexandria. Here he was examined on 15th February 1917 and the board recommended that he return to England. This he did and on 29th March 1917, was posted to the Essex Regimental Depot. He was transferred again on 27th April 1917 to Suffolk Garrison 2nd (Reserve) Battalion.

He was discharged on 25th October 1917 due to sickness (heart problem aggravated by war service) and was issued with Silver War Badge No. 189724. After being examined at Chelsea in September 1917 he was given a pension and re-assessed in January 1919.

In Spring 1919, according to the Electoral Roll, he was living at 6 Oxford Street, Northampton with his wife Phoebe. His family may have moved to be near him when he was based in Northampton.

Family:

Frederick and Phoebe had three children, Edith Ellen (born 1899), Frederick H (1899) and Ellen Lilian (1902).

17th General Hospital, Alexandria C1916

Frederick NASH
(known as Fred)

Nationality:	British
Rank:	Private
Service No:	1522
Regiment:	Oxford and Bucks Light Infantry
Unit:	1/1st Battalion
Age at Death:	32
Date of Death:	30th March 1921
Place of Death:	Northampton
Parents:	Josiah Nash
Wife:	Florence Nash (nee Pratt)
Address:	64 Delapre Street, Far Cotton, Northampton
Grave Ref:	462.1.17934
Medals/Awards:	1915 Star, Victory, British and Silver War Badge

Additional Information:

Fred was born in 1888 in Gravesend. In 1891 he was living at his grandmother's lodging house with his father Josiah (1881 Census Jonah) a bricklayer; and sisters Margaret and Ellen (Nellie), but his mother appears to have died. The lodging house was at Cattle Market, Braintree.

Ten years later the family had moved from the lodging house to New Street, Braintree and were living there with others, including his aunt Sarah.

Fred left school and got a job as a fitter with Crittal & Winterton, ironmongers and was living at 5 Skitts Hill, Braintree. On 15th May 1909 at Braintree he enlisted in the 5th Battalion, Essex Regiment as Private No. 1103. This was a Territorial unit and in late July that year he did his annual training at Worthing. During the following three years he trained at Harwich, Thetford and Shorncliffe in Kent. He listed his sister Mrs Hart as his next of kin.

The 1911 Census showed Fred living with his sister Nellie and working as a hot water fitter at Skitts Hill, Braintree.

In May 1913, he transferred to the 1st Bucks Battalion A Company of the Oxfordshire and Bucks Light Infantry as Private 1522. He was called up on 5th August 1914 at the outbreak of war and went to France with the Battalion (a territorial battalion) on 30th March 1915 as part of South Midlands Brigade. In May 1915 this became the 145th Brigade.

Frederick served in France until 24th December 1915 when he returned to England. He was discharged on 17th May 1916 after serving the full 7 years of engagement and awarded a pension due to a disorderly heart. He was awarded the Silver War Badge No. 151260.

He first lived at 8 Coronation Road, Stony Stratford but later moved to 27 Abbey Road, Far Cotton. This may well have been when he married Florence, in the summer 1916.

Due to his health problem, which he put down to suffering acute stress from strain and exposure in France, he attended Northampton General for examinations. In July 1920 he had an operation for an appendix abscess.

Family:

One daughter Ivy, born 1919.

Rifle Brigade Badge

See David Newton, page 157

David NEWTON

Nationality:	British
Rank:	Private
Service No:	TR/3/14920
Regiment:	The Rifle Brigade
Unit:	19th Battalion (Training Reserve)
Age at Death:	18
Date of Death:	10th May 1917
Place of Death:	Northampton
Parents:	William and Margaret Newton
Grave Ref:	465.1.18030

Additional Information:

David was born about 1898 in Bethnal Green and in 1901 lived at 6 Tuscan Street, Bethnal Green with his father William, a cabinet maker, his mother Margaret and five brothers and sisters. They were still there in 1911 living in five rooms and he had three more brothers.

He attested in August 1916 aged 17 years and 11 months and was put on the Army Reserve. At that time he was living with his mother Margaret at 57 Warley Street, Bethnal Green. His occupation was bill poster and he was 5' 2" tall.

Mobilized on 6th March 1917 in London he was posted to the 19th Training Reserve Battalion of the Rifle Brigade. It later became 237th Graduated Battalion in May 1917. He was vaccinated ready for service on 11th March 1917.

A medical board at Northampton War Hospital (Duston, St Crispin's) on 13th April 1917 found David was physically unfit for military service. He had contracted tuberculosis when at home in London in July 1916. The Board proposed that he be discharged from the army, which he was on 4th May 1917. It was suggested that he be sent to a sanatorium. Six days later David died.

Family:

David had seven siblings, James, William, George, Robert, Harriett, Walter and Joseph. The 1911 Census showed a Lena Newton living in the house, who was a daughter in law; and two grandchildren, William and James.

**Remembrance Sunday Ceremony
All Saints Church, Northampton**

Courtesy of Dave Humphreys

Joseph O'GRADY

Nationality:	British
Rank:	Private
Service No:	PW/771
Regiment:	Duke of Cambridge's Own Middlesex Regiment
Unit:	25th Battalion
Age at Death:	51 (Age stated on death registration)
Date of Death:	4th January 1916
Place of Death:	Northampton
Grave Ref:	449.3.17424

Additional Information:

On 19th March 1915, at Neath, Glamorgan, Joseph enlisted in the army and the following day at Hornsey he joined the Middlesex Regiment. Joseph stated on his attestation paper that he was 44 years old and was born in Mile End. This does not tie with the age given on his death registration record.

The 18th Battalion was also called the 1st Public Works Pioneers and was based at Alexandra Palace (the PW in his number represents Public Works). Joseph transferred to the 19th Battalion on 30th April 1915, also called 2nd Public Works Pioneers. Finally on the 7th August 1915 transferred again to the 25th Reserve Battalion. This Battalion was formed at Tring in 1915 from the Depot companies of 18th, 19th and 26th Battalions and moved to Northampton.

He was taken ill and sent to the Military Hospital Northampton where at 11.25 on the 4th January 1916 he died of acute gastric exhaustion. The Northampton Daily Echo reported that he had previously served in the Munster Fusiliers and was from Poplar.

Family:

Joseph's attestation papers stated that he had no living relatives but this was crossed out and a grandmother, Mrs C Carpenter, living in Poplar was recorded.

John Litchfield PERCIVAL

Nationality:	British
Rank:	Private
Service No:	51091
Regiment:	Royal Army Medical Corps
Age at Death:	26
Date of Death:	20th September 1920
Place of Death:	Northampton
Parents:	Adopted son of Arthur and Annie Gee
Address:	20 Cattle Market Road, Northampton
Grave Ref:	445.3.17296
Medals/Awards:	1914-15 Star, Victory, British and Silver War Badge

Additional Information:

John joined the Royal Army Medical Corps on 3rd September 1914 and went to France on 30th May 1915. He was discharged on 19th October 1918, due to sickness.

The 1901 Census showed that John lived with his mother Alice Percival in Daventry. She was shown as head of the household and the wife of a reservist. Alice died in 1903.

The 1911 Census showed that John lived with his aunt and uncle Arthur and Annie Gee and worked as a boot maker, sewer and stitcher.

Family:

John had five siblings shown on the 1901 Census, George 8, James 4, William 1 (born 1899) and Harry and Tom shown as 8 months. Another brother, John Oliver, was born and died in 1890.

Christopher George PITTAM
(Also shown as George Christopher)

Nationality:	British
Rank:	Private
Service No:	235100
Regiment:	Suffolk
Unit:	Depot F
Age at Death:	19 on death registration, 18 on CWGC
Date of Death:	4th May 1918
Place of Death:	Colchester Registration District
Parents:	George Henry and Louisa Jane Pittam (nee Wall)
Address:	10 St James Street, Northampton
Grave Ref:	447.4.17369
Medals/Awards:	Victory and British

Additional Information:

Christopher enlisted at Bedford but no records exist. One source stated that he died of wounds. Christopher was baptised on 4th December 1898 which, if he was baptised when a few months old, makes his age at death 19.

The 1911 Census showed Christopher lived with his parents at 10 St James Street, Northampton and his father worked in a brewery.

The Northampton Daily Echo reported that Christopher was the son of Mr & Mrs Pittam of 10 St James Street and was seriously wounded in France. He died at Colchester Hospital after having his arm amputated.

Family:

Christopher had six siblings, Ivy, Mabel, Sydney, Horace, Doris and Gladys.

Arthur Ernest PITTAMS

Nationality:	British
Rank:	Private
Service No:	111726
Regiment:	Royal Fusiliers
Unit:	44th Battalion
Age at Death:	24
Date of Death:	17th February 1919
Place of Death:	Northampton
Parents:	Charles and Annie Pittams (nee Tookey)
Wife:	Ivy May Pittams (nee Watkins)
Address:	72 Hood Street, Northampton
Grave Ref:	445.4.17305
Medals/Awards:	Victory and British

Additional Information:

Arthur was born in Piddington where his father Charles, according to the 1901 Census, was a publican and coal dealer. By 1911 Arthur worked as a farm labourer. He had four service numbers which were GS/26533 Royal Fusiliers; 67587 Suffolk Regiment; 609686 Labour Corps; and finally 111726 Royal Fusiliers. The 43rd and 44th Garrison Battalions formed in France in May and September 1918 from Garrison Guard Companies for duty at Army Headquarters. They were manned by troops who had been rated as medically unfit for front line duty.

Arthur married Ivy in 1916 but no children can be found.

Family:

Arthur had six siblings but one had died by the time of the 1911 Census. The remaining siblings were William, Martha, Sarah, Sidney and Reuben.

Reuben was working as a milkman in 1918. Rueben appeared in front of the Military Tribunal in May 1918. He was given temporary exemption until 31st August 1918. He may have appealed again, or have been called up, but he was very unlikely to have seen active service.

George REEVE

Nationality:	British
Rank:	Lieutenant
Service No:	7574
Regiment:	Royal Irish Fusiliers
Attached to:	King's Royal Rifle Corps (KRRC)
Age at Death:	32
Date of Death:	15th October 1918
Place of Death:	Colchester
Parents:	George and Lydia Reeve (nee White)
Address:	15 King Street, Northampton (parents)
Grave Ref:	446.3.17328
Medals/Awards:	Military Cross, Military Medal, 1914 Star, Victory and British

Additional Information:

George was born in Spratton, Northamptonshire in 1886 and christened on 24th October 1886. The 1891 Census showed him living with his parents and one sister in 3 Bakers Lane, Spratton. His father was a labourer. The 1901 Census showed that the family still lived in Spratton with four more children and his father was then an ironstone labourer. The 1911 Census showed that George and Lydia Reeve (his parents) lived at 15 King Street, Northampton with two more children.   15 King Street was the address shown on the medal card for the 1914 Star to be dispatched.

There are two George Reeve's on the 1911 Census with Northampton as their birthplace but it is not possible to identify which is the right one.

George's service in the Royal Irish Fusiliers was one of great distinction. First entering France on 22nd August 1914, he was wounded in action at least four times, commissioned in the field for gallantry and awarded the M.C. and M.M. George served in the front line throughout the war from Mons in 1914 until early 1918 apart from periods when he was recovering from wounds.

Notice of his Military Medal was published in the London Gazette on 11th November 1916.   The regimental history states that this medal was presented by the General Officer Commanding 4th Division at Ercourt on 26th November 1916, together with medals to 14 other men of the battalion, all awarded for "gallantry and good service up at Ypres in 1915".

The citation for his Military Cross, published in the London Gazette on 18th July 1917 reads:

"For conspicuous gallantry and devotion to duty.   He showed great resource and determination in assuming command of his company when all other officers were casualties, in reorganising men of other companies, in digging in and maintaining his position. He subsequently withdrew with his flanks in the air and brought all his wounded with him. His skill was most marked."

The Battalion War Diary for 3rd May 1917 stated: "At about 4.25 am 'A' and 'B' Coys. got held up on the near side of the Roeux-Gravrelle Road by heavy machine-gun fire from the chemical works, a house south of them and also from the buildings north of the Chateau and the Chateau itself.   This forced 'A' Coy, across 'B's front and Reeve although wounded, collected all Irish Fusiliers, reorganised them, and dug in on a line from West of the Chateau to the railway embankment, where he established himself and remained until recalled by order at 10.10 pm.

He succeeded in withdrawing with few casualties bringing his wounded with him."

On 5th November 1917 George had the unenviable task of commanding the firing party responsible for executing Private G Hanna of the 1st Battalion, Royal Irish Fusiliers.

George's medal card showed that at one time he held the rank of Serjeant. He was promoted to Acting Regimental Serjeant Major on 19th April 1915 and on 30th November 1915 the war diary records him joining for duty as a Lieutenant. He was promoted to full Lieutenant on 5th February 1918.

George was wounded on several occasions. The first known being 18th January 1916, when he was wounded in the right leg. He returned to England on 18th February 1916 and returned to his Battalion on 14th July 1916. On 12th October 1916 he received a gunshot to his left leg and suffered shell shock. He was sent to England on 19th October 1916 and must have returned to his Battalion before the presentation of his Military Medal on 16th November 1916.

George was again wounded on 3rd May 1917 but remained on duty. He was admitted to the 11th Field Ambulance on 2nd August 1917 and returned to duty on 22nd August 1917 re-joining his Battalion on 30th August 1917. The records show he was wounded on 5th February 1918 and returned to duty on 12th February 1918. He was wounded, as far as can be ascertained, for the last time on 8th March 1918.

Late in 1918, probably as a result of his wounds, Reeves was attached to the 52nd Battalion, K.R.R.C. based at Colchester, Essex. Tragically, on 14th October 1918, whilst walking towards Colchester from the Goojerat Barracks, he was struck by a taxi and died in hospital early the following morning.

Family:

George had seven siblings, Kate, Emma, Richard H, Samuel, Sydney P, Florence and Frank. Richard appears to have survived the war and may have died in 1947.

Samuel (Sam) served, as Private No. 15922, in the 7th Battalion of the Northamptonshire Regiment and died on 17th August 1916, aged 20. He is commemorated on the Thiepval Memorial.

Sydney (Sidney) Phillip served as Private No. 36728, in the 8th Battalion, East Surrey Regiment and was listed as missing on 19th May 1918. He is recorded as having died on 22nd May 1918, aged 19. He is buried at the Pernois British Cemetery, Halloy-les-Pernois.

Sources:

Baptism records and auction catalogue (in September 2001 George Reeve's MC and MM came up for auction at DNW, London).

Book, *Researching British Military Medals* by Steve Dymond

Royal Irish Fusiliers Museum Sovereign's House, The Mall, Armagh, BT61 9DL www.royal-irish.com

Joseph RIDDLE

Nationality:	British
Rank:	Serjeant
Service No:	12665
Regiment:	Machine Gun Corps (Infantry)
Unit:	2nd Battalion
Age at Death:	41
Date of Death:	13th May 1917
Place of Death:	Southwell, Nottinghamshire Registration District
Parents:	Joseph and Sarah Riddle of Rushden
Wife:	Mary Ann Riddle
Address:	41 Gladstone Terrace, Northampton
Grave Ref:	448.3.17384

Additional Information:

Joseph was born in Ware, Hertfordshire and his family were still there at the time of the 1881 Census. His father, Joseph, was listed as a brickfield labourer and there were four children, including Joseph aged 6. The mother's name was listed as Emma but there is no death listed for an Emma Riddle between this Census and the next in 1891 and no marriage of a Joseph to a Sarah.

1891 Census showed Joseph and his parents still in Ware and his father was working as a labourer and his mother as a charwoman. There were two more children. Joseph served on the North West Frontier (India) from 1897-1898.

The 1901 Census showed Joseph working as a bargeman as was his father. Their address was given as West Hampstead and Joseph had two more siblings.

By the time of the 1911 Census Joseph was married to Mary Ann Draycott and this marriage took place in the Spring of 1910 in Northampton. They lived at 9 St. Andrews Gardens, St Andrews Street, Northampton and Joseph worked as a carter. No children could be traced from this marriage.

Joseph's records show that he served in the Northants Regiment as No.10307 and must subsequently have transferred to the Machine Gun Corps.

Family:

Joseph's siblings were Ellen, Walter, Rose, Nellie, Henry, Mabel and Robert.

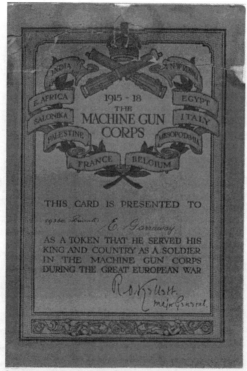

Courtesy of Anne Garraway

Scroll presented to each member of the Machine Gun Corps who served in the First World War

Arthur ROBINSON

Nationality:	British
Rank:	Private
Service No:	45754
Regiment:	Royal Defence Corps
Unit:	19th Battalion
Age at Death:	23
Date of Death:	3rd December 1918
Place of Death:	Northampton
Parents:	Mary Robinson
Grave Ref:	445.2.17307

Additional Information:

It would seem that Arthur was transferred to the 682nd Agricultural Company of the Labour Corps with the service no. 441729.

The only Arthur Robinson that seems to match this man was, in 1901 in the Cottage Homes, Burton Latimer (see photo page 170). These were homes for children who otherwise would have been in the Kettering Workhouse. Over 100 children were accommodated in the Cottage Homes. Arthur was registered at Finedon Road Infants School where his parent/guardian's name was given as Mary and date of birth 7th November 1895. He was a prize winner at the Finedon Road Infants School in 1900 and received a price for regular attendance at their Sunday School in 1902/3.

In 1911, Arthur was still at the Cottage Homes, aged 15, and assisting in the garden. On 11th September 1911, the Guardians' Minutes showed that "Arthur Robinson to go to J Webb, coal and coke merchant, Irthlingborough on a month's trial". On 18th December 1911 the record showed that "Arthur Robinson satisfactory and to remain with Mr Webb at Irthlingborough".

Source: www.burtonlatimer.info.history/Cottagehomes.html

George ROBINSON

Nationality:	British
Rank:	Private
Service No:	25277
Regiment:	Royal Defence Corps
Unit:	100th Company
Age at Death:	53
Date of Death:	21st February 1917
Place of Death:	Northampton
Grave Ref:	448.2.17395

Additional Information:

The internet dataset 'Soldiers who Died in the Great War' states that George was born in Escrick and enlisted in Selby. This cannot be verified. No medal card has been found.

A report of George's funeral stated that his home was Pattishall and that he died at Duston War Hospital.

The 1911 Census showed a George Robinson aged 46 born in Escrick, living at Chapel Yard, Selby. He was shown as married but there are no other occupants of the house. He was working as a labourer. The 1901 Census showed a Corporal George Robinson, aged 34, of the Royal Garrison Regiment, living with his parents Joseph and Jane in Escrick. Whilst we have been unable to verify this is the right George Robinson these entries seem the correct fit.

Cottage Homes Burton Latimer (see Arthur Robinson)

William ROSS

Nationality: British
Rank: Gunner
Service No: 59307
Regiment: Royal Garrison Artillery
Age at Death: 41
Date of Death: 23rd October 1917
Grave Ref: 464.1.18022
Medals/Awards: Victory and British

Additional Information:

It would appear that William moved through various regiments. He was Private No. 37023 in the Hampshire Regiment, No.108364 in the Labour Corps and finally 59307 in the Royal Garrison Artillery.

The dataset 'Soldiers who Died in the Great War' stated that William was born in Leamside, Co. Durham, and was living at Littleburn Colliery, Durham at the time of his enlistment in North Shields. No census records can be found which match this information.

The only death registration that seems to match is for Christchurch Registration District but the age is given as 38.

The funeral of Reginald Clarence Scanes

Reginald Clarence SCANES

Nationality:	Australian
Rank:	Private
Service No:	2975
Regiment:	Australian Infantry (AIF)
Unit:	53rd Battalion
Age at Death:	23
Date of Death:	6th May 1918
Place of Death:	Northampton
Parents:	Samuel and Margaret Scanes (nee Kirk)
Address:	7 Malcolm Street, Erskineville, New South Wales
Grave Ref:	447.3.17368
Medals/Awards:	Victory and British

Additional Information:

Reginald was born in Cooma, New South Wales in 1894. He enlisted on 1st May 1916 at Erskineville, Sydney and gave his occupation as a mail driver.

He reported to Dubbo Camp on 23rd June 1916 and moved to a training camp in July. He embarked in Sydney on board Troop Transport Ship Ascanius on 25th October 1916 and arrived in Devonport on 28th December 1916. He left for France on 14th June 1917 and was taken onto the strength of the 53rd Battalion on 1st July 1917. He had leave in England from 24th February 1918 to 12th March 1918.

He was wounded in action on 17th April 1918. He was transferred on 19th April, via a clearing station to 11th Stationary Hospital, Rouen, suffering gas poisoning. He was admitted to Northampton War Hospital Duston and died of gas gangrene and septic pneumonia on 6th May 1918.

His funeral was attended by a number of his comrades, a Miss McKinnell, Mr Parkinson and Miss Mabel Parkinson. Miss McKinnell was listed in a newspaper report of his funeral as the Australian Official Visitor. A letter from Mabel was found in his possessions and as Mabel was only 19 it might be assumed she was his sweetheart.

The newspaper report also stated that "the flower card and regimental ribbon of green and black from each comrade's wreath are to be sent to Private Scanes's mother in Australia".

The photograph in the newspaper dated 18th May 1918 showed about 20 Australian soldiers following his coffin at the funeral (see picture on page 171).

There was a letter on file from a Gertrude MacKinnell, a member of the Red Cross. On the 1911 Census there was a Gertrude Clare McKinnell, aged 41, daughter of a local chemist.

Family:

Reginald had six siblings, Hannah, Samuel, Frederick, Lilly, Mabel and Albert.

Source: Picture of Reginald courtesy of Ron and Murray Kirkland. Murray, his great nephew, has produced a triptych of this and two other photographs which is displayed at the Australian War Memorial in Canberra. www.murraykirkland.co.au

Arthur Thomas SEAL
(served as Arthur COOK)

Nationality:	British
Rank:	Serjeant
Service No:	13675
Regiment:	Duke of Cornwall's Light Infantry
Unit:	6th Battalion
Age at Death:	26
Date of Death:	6th October 1916
Place of Death:	Chelmsford
Parents:	Son of Katrina Cook (formerly Seal nee Beck) and Thomas Seal (deceased)
Address:	84 Louise Road, Northampton (mother's address)
Grave Ref:	466.1.18062
Medals/Awards:	Military Medal, 1915 Star, Victory and British

Additional Information:

Arthur was born in Northampton in 1890 and his parents were Kate Beck and Thomas Arthur Seal. On the 1891 Census, Arthur only 9 months old, lived with his parents at 31 Western Road, Leicester and his father worked as a boot finisher aged 28. His mother was aged 22 and both his parents were shown as being born in Northampton. Arthur's father, Thomas, died in the December quarter 1899 in Northampton.

The 1901 Census showed Arthur living with his mother and her new partner Albert Cook and his three siblings at 24 Greyfriars, Northampton. His mother, Kate, and all the children were shown with the surname Cook. Albert was a cattle dealer. On the 1911 Census Arthur, still using the surname Cook, was shown as a boarder at 98 Euston Road, Far Cotton, Northampton and he worked as a loco engine cleaner.

Arthur served under the name of Cook and his death is recorded under both surnames on the CWGC database.

Arthur enlisted at Finsbury Barrack, London on 1st September 1914. He was posted to the 6th Service Battalion of the Duke of Cornwall's Light

Infantry which was in the process of being established in a tented camp at Watt's Common, Aldershot. On 21st May 1915 he left England with the 6th Battalion landing at Boulogne on 22nd May. The 6th Battalion was part of the 43rd Light Infantry Brigade. Arthur was part of the advance party.

In its early days on the Western Front the Battalion was deployed in the Ypres Salient, taking part in the battles of Hooge and Sanctuary Wood. However, on 14th July 1916 it moved south to the Somme where the great battles had been raging since 1st July. Between 15th and 30th July it was heavily involved in the infamous battle of Delville Wood, in which it lost 14 officers and 283 soldiers killed and wounded. Between 15th September and 22nd September, it fought in the battle of Flers-Courcelette where, out of its remaining strength of 20 officers and 550 soldiers, it lost a further 15 officers and 294 soldiers killed and wounded.

It is most likely that Thomas was wounded during the battle at Flers-Courcelette and earned his bravery award as a result of his efforts during those days.

The London Gazette published on 20th October 1916, Issue No. 29794, page 10216 listed his Military Medal but under the name of Cook.

The CWGC stated Arthur died of his wounds.

Family:

Arthur had three siblings, Reuben Victor (born 1891) Gertrude L (1894) and Ethel Grace (1896). All the births were registered under the surname Seal.

Source: Cornwall's Regimental Museum, The Keep, Bodmin, Cornwall, PL31 1EG. www.cornwall-regimentalmuseum.org

Glynn SEPHTON

Nationality:	British
Rank:	Private
Service No:	78972
Regiment:	Tank Corps
Unit:	Depot
Age at Death:	27
Date of Death:	2nd December 1918
Place of Death:	The Military Hospital, Scotton, Yorkshire (Catterick Camp)
Parents:	Joseph and Clara Sephton (nee Cumberland)
Wife:	Dorothy Rachel Sephton (nee Pollard)
Address:	9 Southampton Road, Far Cotton, Northampton
Grave Ref:	161.2.6278
Medals/Awards:	Victory and British

Additional Information:

Glynn was first mentioned on the 1891 Census aged 1 month. His parents were aged 34 and 30 and he had an older sister Lilly aged 4. Joseph, his father, was working as a railway clerk and was born in Warrington. His mother Clara was born in Houghton Regis. They were living at 1a Abbey Road, Hardingstone.

Glynn joined the railway service in 1906 as a Clerk at Bicester Goods Yard and moved to Iron Bridge Light Goods on 2nd August 1912. He was shown on the railway personnel records as 'OHMS' on 25th October 1916. This is presumed to be the date he joined the forces.

On the 1911 Census Glynn was living with his mother Clara at 61 Delapre Street, Far Cotton, Northampton and worked as a railway clerk. There was no mention of his father but his mother was not shown as a widow. 61 Delapre Street, Far Cotton was shown in the 1910 and 1914 Kelly's Directory as a Post Office and Newsagents.

Glynn married Dorothy in the September quarter of 1916 in the Hardingstone Registration District.

His will went through probate and was advertised in 1919. He left his estate to Dorothy and it had a value of £253 18s 8d (£253.91). Her address was given as 127 Southampton Road, Northampton.

Glyn was buried in a family grave just outside the war graves section.

Sources: Baker Family Tree on Ancestry.co.uk

The Mark IV Tank as used at Cambrai in November 1917

John SIMS

Nationality:	British
Rank:	Private
Service No:	265528
Regiment:	Monmouthshire Regiment
Unit:	2nd Battalion
Age at Death:	48 on Registration and cemetery record but likely to be 45
Date of Death:	31st October 1918
Place of Death:	Leicester
Parents:	William and Ellen Sims (nee Spillane)
Wife:	Isabella Sims (nee Morris)
Address:	21 Oak Street, Cwmbran
Grave Ref:	446.4.17321
Medals/Awards:	1914 Star, Victory, British and Silver War Badge

Additional Information:

On the 1881 Census John was living with his parents at 16 Nightingale Row, Upper Llanvrechva, and his father was a labourer in an iron works. By 1891 he was living with his mother at Forge Hammond, Cwmbran.

John enlisted in the 1st Cheshire Regiment on 25th August 1892, at Brecon, as Private No. 3839. On 17th February 1894 he went to India to join the 1st Battalion Cheshire Regiment already based there. He served for 10 years in India having extended his service to 12 years while there. He returned home just in time to retire on 29th November 1904. During his service he was awarded three Good Conduct badges.

He may have re-enlisted as he cannot be found on the 1911 Census and his medal card stated that he was retired on 29th July 1912.

He re-enlisted on 29th August 1914 at Pontypool where he had been working as a labourer at the local power station. He joined the Monmouthshire Regiment as Private No. 2228 from National Reserve and was posted to France on 7th November 1914 but returned to the UK very quickly on 24th November and remained "at home" until 14th March 1918 when he was discharged as unfit.

He gave his next of kin as his brother Jeremiah Sims at 21 Oak Street. The almost illegible doctor's report seemed to indicate that John may have been sick for some time. The indication was that he had heart problems.

He was said to be of good character, sober, steady and industrious. He was given Silver War Badge No. B151937. He indicated that he was going to live at 118 Stanhope Road, Northampton.

Family:

John married Isabella in the September quarter 1915 in Northampton.

John's mother had been married before marrying his father and there is a half-brother Thomas Ellsmore and a half sister Mary Ann. John had four siblings, Polly, Mary, Jeremiah, and Ellen.

Courtesy of the Imperial War Museum

Wounded Canadians being moved from Courcelette in the autumn of 1916.

Benjamin SLATER

Nationality:	Canadian
Rank:	Private
Service No:	124620
Regiment:	Princess Patricia's Canadian Light Infantry (Eastern Ontario)
Age at Death:	24
Date of Death:	26th September 1916
Place of Death:	Northampton
Wife:	Hattie Slater
Address:	387 Glebe Street, London, Ontario (at Attestation)
Grave Ref:	466.1.18066

Additional Information:

Benjamin attested on 12th January 1916 at London, Ontario, Canada. He gave his date of birth as 21st March 1892 in Burnley, Lancashire, England. His occupation was given as a weaver.

Benjamin's original overseas unit was 70th Canadian Infantry Battalion. He joined the Princess Patricia's Canadian Light Infantry in the field on 9th June 1916. He was wounded at the battle of Flers-Courcelette.

Flers-Courcelette was part of the battle of the Somme and was one of the first actions to use a rolling barrage and tanks. In an action that began at dawn, the Canadian Corps assaulted on a two-kilometre front. By the time the action finished it had suffered 24,029 casualties. Lloyd George wrote that the Canadians "played a part of such distinction that thenceforward they were marked out as storm troops. .... Whenever the Germans found the Canadian Corps coming into the line they prepared for the worst".

See picture on page 179 of Canadian soldiers being moved by light railway, pulled by a horse, from the battle site.

Ellis Victor Ashby SMITH

Nationality:	British
Rank:	Private
Service No:	28965
Regiment:	Essex Regiment
Unit:	14th Battalion
Transferred to:	98th Battalion Training Reserve (TR10/36432)
Age at Death:	28
Date of Death:	13th January 1917
Place of Death:	Coatbridge, Lanarkshire
Parents:	Thomas Edward and Mercy Ann Smith (nee Ashby)
Wife:	Evelyn Emmie Smith (nee Old)
Address:	7 Rickard Street, Far Cotton, Northampton
Grave Ref:	321.1.12512 – Just outside War Grave Section

Additional Information:

The 1901 Census showed Ellis living with his parents at Church Street, Rothersthorpe. His father was a labourer born in Brafield on the Green. His mother was born in Rothersthorpe. The 1911 Census showed that Ellis still lived with his parents and worked as a blast furnace labourer.

Ellis attested in December 1915 and at that time lived at 14 Oxford Street, Northampton and his occupation was a shunter. He was transferred to the Reserves and was sent to the Gartsherrier Iron Works at Coatbridge owned by William Baird & Co. He was run over by a wagon and death was certified as instantaneous.

After the accident there was some correspondence between the owners of the iron works and the army about who was responsible for the family's expenses and the transfer of his coffin to Northampton. Correspondence then followed as to whether his widow was entitled to a pension. The Army considered that he was not an active soldier and therefore no pension was applicable from "public funds".

Family:

Ellis had six siblings, John who died in 1912, Emma, Thomas, Vincent, Amelia and Percy.

Evelyn and Ellis had two children at the time of his death, Leslie and Ernest.

Gartsherrier Iron Works, Coatbridge

James SMITH

Nationality:	British
Rank:	Private
Service No:	23808 and 59953
Regiment:	1st Northamptonshire
Age at Death:	29
Date of Death:	7th December 1923
Place of Death:	Luton Registration District
Grave Ref:	462.17930
Medals/Awards:	Victory, British and Silver War Badge

Additional Information:

James was called up on 23rd March 1916 and served in France. He was discharged on 3rd April 1919 due to sickness being awarded Silver War Badge No. 1444.

This death was not recorded on the Commonwealth War Graves Commission site as his death was after 31st August 1921.

Apart from this we have been unable to identify any other information about James.

Victory Medal

The ribbon has a 'two rainbow' design with violet from each rainbow on the outside edges moving to a central red stripe

(For further information see Campaign Medals and Awards at page 221)

Kenneth George SMITH

Nationality:	British
Rank:	Aircraftman 2nd Class
Service No:	1192756
Regiment:	Royal Air Force
Unit:	Volunteer Reserve
Age at Death:	20
Date of Death:	22nd February 1941
Place of Death:	Barnstaple Registration District
Parents:	Cyril and Fanny Smith
Address:	Northampton
Grave Ref:	445.17277

Additional Information:

Kenneth would appear to have been born in the Towcester Registration District and his mother's maiden name was Coy. If that is correct his father's full name is Cyril J B Smith and these are the initials of a Cyril James Banyard Smith born 1891 in Towcester from a large family of wheelwrights.

The Northampton Daily Chronicle reported that Kenneth died at RAF Chivenor from pneumonia. They also reported that he was the son of Mr C Smith and brother of Leslie of 83 Charles Street, Northampton.

Family:

Kenneth had five siblings, Leslie, Ronald, Frederick, Gerald and Joyce.

Levi SMITH

Nationality:	British
Rank:	Private
Service No:	PW/2341
Regiment:	Middlesex
Unit:	25th Battalion
Age at Death:	40
Date of Death:	9th April 1916
Place of Death:	Northampton
Wife:	Annie Smith (nee Parkinson)
Address:	17 Hopwood Place, Rochdale
Grave Ref:	448.4.17413

Additional Information:

The first record of Levi is on the 1911 Census when he had been married to Annie for three years. He was an outdoor labourer and they had no children. He gave his place of birth as Coates, Cambridgeshire but no birth record can be found.

Levi enlisted on 5th May 1915 and there is no record of him leaving the UK. According to a report in the Derby Daily Telegraph, he was the servant of Colonel John Ward MP and had an accident to his hand when starting the Colonel's car. He was admitted to hospital on 5th April and died on the 9th from septic poisoning.

Colonel Ward described Levi as a "man of high character and one of the most faithful servants a man could have. In civil life I should call him my friend and, but for King's Regulations, would do so now".

Family:

His papers showed him as having no living parents, grandparents or siblings, though there was mention of a brother John on one document. Annie remarried in December 1916 to a Samuel Moore.

Walter SMITH

Nationality:	British
Rank:	Private
Service No:	2494
Regiment:	1/4th Northants Regiment
Also served in:	Labour Corps (548574)
Age at Death:	36
Date of Death:	18th November 1921
Place of Death:	Hardingstone Registration District
Grave Ref:	462.17291
Medals/Awards:	1915 Star, Victory and British

Additional Information:

Walter entered the theatre of war on 10th August 1915. The medal card had No. 3 in the box beside "theatre of war first served in" which meant he served in Egypt.

As there were several men with the name Walter Smith, who had Northampton connections, it was not possible to identify his family or verify the correct enlistment or pension record.

British War Medal 1914-1920

Ribbon has a central orange stripe flanked by two narrow white stripes, two black stripes and on the outside edge a blue stripe

(For further information see Campaign Medals and Awards page 221)

James SNEDKER

Nationality:	British
Rank:	Rifleman
Service No:	5703
Regiment:	London (London Irish Rifles)
Unit:	2/18th Battalion
Age at Death:	25
Date of Death:	27th October 1918
Place of Death:	Northampton
Parents:	George and Mary Snedker
Address:	26 Lower Hester Street, Northampton
Grave Ref:	446.3.17324
Medals/Awards:	Victory and British, Silver War Badge 49114

Additional Information:

The 1901 Census showed James lived with his parents in Brook Street, Northampton and his father was a shoe finisher.

James, together with his siblings Elsie, Dora, Bertha, and their father George were admitted to the Workhouse on 4th July 1906. George was shown as married and destitute. The children were discharged to Scattered Homes (see note on Frederick Deacon) on 6th July 1906. George was discharged on 14th July, at his own request.

On the 1911 Census James was living with his parents at 26 Lower Hester Street and he worked as a shoe finisher.

James enlisted on 25th October 1915 in Northampton and was posted to the 18th London Regiment. There was a mention of the Royal Army Medical Corps on his record but this was unclear.

He was posted to France on 24th June 1916 and was severely wounded at Neuville St Vaust on 9th October 1916. He received a rifle bullet wound which entered his left temple and exited through his right eye. Both eyes had to be removed.

He was immediately returned home and was discharged medically unfit for duty on 8th January 1917. He received a pension of 25s (£1.25) weekly for life. In July 1917 an attendance allowance of £1 per week was paid to one of his sisters. On 16th July 1918 this was reviewed and again granted as "man dangerously ill and unlikely to live more than a few weeks".

James died at home.

Family:

James had 9 siblings, Florence, Walter, Ethel, Ada, Elsie, Bertha, Dora, John and George.

Florence's husband George Wells was also buried in the Commonwealth War Graves section of Towcester Road Cemetery having died on 2nd October 1918. (see page 201)

AUSTRALIAN WAR MEMORIAL   H1310:

This early photograph of Towcester Road Cemetery shows the grave of James Snedker on the left front row and George Campbell Easton on the right front row (biography on page 80).

188

John H SOUTHWORTH

Rank:	Private
Service No:	R/4/063567
Regiment:	Royal Army Service Corps
Unit:	Remounts
Age at Death:	45 (death registration)
Date of Death:	24th February 1919
Place of Death:	Northampton
Parents:	Henry and Betsy Southworth (nee Bridge)
Wife:	Mary Ellen Southworth (nee Taylor)
Address:	20 Argo Street, Bolton, Lancs
Grave Ref:	445.3.17304

Additional Information:

The 1881 Census showed John living with his parents together with several siblings, including his twin sister Mary Jane. By 1891 four more siblings had been born. John married Mary on 10th October 1896 at St Saviour's Church, Bolton.

By the time of the 1901 Census John and Mary were living in Bamber Street, Bolton and he gave his occupation as groom/cab driver. At the time of the 1911 Census John and Mary were living at 87 Morris Green Lane, Bolton and he described himself as a carter.

John attested on 8th April 1915 and he gave his address as 20 Argo Street, Bolton. He stated he was 36 years and 330 days old, and a groom. He was posted to the Remounts and transferred to Kettering on 19th August 1916. His record showed that he died at Duston War Hospital of a malignant carcinoma in his neck.

Family:

John had ten siblings, Margaret (born 1871), Mary Jane, his twin (1874), Alice (1876), Walter (1877), Emily 1879), Herbert (1881) Frederick (1883), Harry (1885), Percy (1887) and Stanley (1889).

John and Mary had three children, Albert (born 1898), Ruth (1901) and Alice (1908).

Percy STOCKER

Nationality:	British
Rank:	Gunner
Service No:	90584
Regiment:	Royal Field Artillery
Unit:	"D" Battery, 256th Brigade
Age at Death:	20
Date of Death:	20th November 1918
Place of Death:	Northampton
Parents:	Alice Stocker and Henry Stocker (deceased)
Address:	3 Charles Street, Northampton
Grave Ref:	446.2.17315
Medals/Awards:	Victory and British

Additional Information:

The 1901 Census showed Percy living with his grandmother Susannah Holiday and his mother Alice Susannah Stocker who worked as a charwomen. Henry, his father, had died in 1898. By 1911 Percy and his family lived in Weston Favell and his mother still worked as a charwoman. Percy was at school. Before enlistment Percy had worked as a stableman in the goods yard, at Northampton, for the Midland Railway Co.

A newspaper report of Percy's funeral stated that he was called up in August 1915 and first went to the front in January 1916. He had been brought to Duston Hospital in October of 1918 with wounds to his back and left shoulder.

At the outbreak of the war men of the Midland Railway Co. were quick to enlist and by the 18th November 1914, 7,531 were at war. By the end of the war this had reached 22,941, which was 30.9% of the workforce. Of these men 2,833 died; 7,068 wounded and 738 taken prisoner. (source: www.midlandrailwaystudycentre.org.uk)

Family:

Percy had two older siblings, Henry and Beatrice.

Henry enlisted into the Northamptonshire Regiment in August 1914 as Private No. 128681. He was wounded twice in 1916 and was transferred to light duties. He married Ada in November 1917.

Typical group of patients and nurses at Duston Hospital

Leslie Charles SUMMERFORD
(known as Les)

Nationality:	British
Rank:	Private
Service No:	5891368
Regiment:	Northamptonshire
Unit:	70th Battalion
Age at Death:	18
Date of Death:	27th November 1941
Place of Death:	Truro
Parents:	William Charles and Emily Ellen Summerford (nee Allum)
Address:	Far Cotton, Northampton
Grave Ref:	461.17914

Additional Information:

The Northampton Daily Chronicle contained a notice stating that Leslie was the only son of William and brother of Muriel and Joan. Grandson of Mrs A. Mrs A is probably Agnes E Summerford mother of William and grandmother of Leslie.

The 70th Battalion was a training and airfield defence unit.

Alfred Robert SWANN

Nationality:	British
Rank:	Serjeant
Service No:	157
Regiment:	Northamptonshire
Unit:	1/4th Battalion
Age at Death:	39
Date of Death:	6th December 1915
Place of Death:	Registered Nottingham
Parents:	William and Martha Swann
Wife:	Emily Swann (nee Barnes)
Address:	124 Green Street, Northampton
Grave Ref:	449.3.17428
Medals/Awards:	1915 Star, British and Victory

Additional Information:

Alfred was shown as living with his parents on the 1881 and 1891 Census. By the time he was 14 he was working as a shoe clicker. On the 1911 Census, he was married to Emily and working as an edge setter, boot finisher. They had five children of which four were still living.

1/4th Battalion of the Northamptonshire Regiment embarked from Liverpool in July 1915 and landed at Suvla Bay, Gallipoli, on 15th August 1915. It was evacuated to Alexandria on 19th December 1915 and spent the rest of the war in Egypt and Palestine.

Alfred went with the 1/4th Battalion of the Northamptonshire Regiment from Liverpool to Suvla Bay. While in Gallipoli he contracted jaundice and was sent to hospital in Malta in November 1915. From there he appears to have been sent back to England where he died.

He had 22 years service in the Territorials.

A newspaper report of his death, stated that "he had contracted dysentery in the Dardannelles. He was a stalwart and smart soldier whose death will be greatly regretted by his comrades. .... Sergt. Swann was working at Messrs Padmore and Barnes when he was called to the colours at the outbreak of the war".

The death of his widow Emily, who died on 12th November 1959, aged 85, was commemorated on Alfred's headstone.

Family:

Alfred had eight siblings, Sarah, Jane, Harry, Frank, William, Kate, Annie and Arthur.

His children were Harry, Florence, Lois, Alfred and Robert born in the December Quarter 1915. There was another birth recorded of a Frank in Market Bosworth in 1912 with the same parental surnames.

Alfred's son, Harry, served in the same battalion as Corporal No. 200198, at Gallipoli with his father. He transferred with the 1/4th Battalion to Egypt and Palestine where he died, aged 20, on 19th April 1917. He was buried at Gaza War Cemetery. He was awarded the 1915 Star, British and Victory Medals.

John William TAGGART

Nationality:	British
Rank:	Private
Service No:	7452
Regiment:	North Staffordshire
Unit:	1st Battalion
Age at Death:	42 (40 on death registration)
Date of Death:	12th July 1916
Place of Death:	Northampton
Grave Ref:	448.3.17408
Medals/Awards:	1914 Star and clasp, Victory and British

Additional Information:

The dataset 'Soldiers who Died in the Great War' states that John was born in Liverpool and enlisted at Crewe. It also gives John's residence as Calke, Staffordshire.

There was a John William Taggart recorded on the 1911 Census as being in India with the North Staffordshire Regiment. He was a Private, unmarried and born in Liverpool. The 1901 Census recorded a John Taggart, born in Liverpool, living with his sister and brother-in-law in Audley, Staffordshire.

John's medal card showed that he entered the Theatre of War on 10th September 1914. The clasp indicates that he served 'under fire of the enemy. He died at Duston War Hospital.

Albert Edward TIBBS

Nationality:	British
Rank:	Private
Service No:	72378
Regiment:	Royal Army Medical Corps
Unit:	104th Field Ambulance
Age at Death:	38
Date of Death:	10th January 1917
Place of Death:	Northampton
Parents:	John and Mary Ann Tibbs
Wife:	Florence Lavinia Tibbs (nee Liddington)
Address:	42 Clinton Road, Far Cotton, Northampton
Grave Ref:	187.3.7204
Medals/Awards:	Victory and British

Additional Information:

Albert was born in Bugbrooke and on the 1881 Census he lived with his parents. His father worked as a labourer in an iron furnace. By 1901 Albert lived in Royston working on the railways but the 1911 Census found him back in Northampton living with his wife and children at 42 Clinton Road. They were sharing the house with Florence's parents. Albert worked as a furnace labourer. Florence and Albert had been married for four years and had already lost one child.

Albert enlisted on 15th October 1915 giving his father as his next of kin. On the 10th August 1916 he was admitted to the London Hospital, Denmark Hill, having been returned from France. He was stated to be dangerously ill. He appeared to have suffered from bronchitis together with tuberculosis.

He was sent to Welford Road Hospital, Northampton on 22nd September 1916 and declared permanently unfit.

Family:

Albert had seven siblings, William, Emily, John, Rose, Ada, Margaret and Oliver.

Florence, his wife who he married in 1906, died in 1913 before he enlisted. His children, Frances (aged 9) and Doris (6), at the time of his death, were left in the guardianship of their grandparents Joseph and Elizabeth Liddington.

Albert is buried outside the
Commonwealth War Grave Section

William TIDY
(alternate spelling Tidey)

Nationality:	British
Rank:	Driver
Service No:	133291
Regiment:	Royal Field Artillery
Unit:	62nd Division Ammunition Company
Age at Death:	22 (CWGC states 20)
Date of Death:	14th December 1916
Place of Death:	Northampton
Parents:	Albert and Harriet Tidey (nee Underwood)
Wife:	Rose Rossi (formerly Tidey nee Lemon)
Address:	13 George Street, Hamilton, Ontario, Canada
Grave Ref:	465.1.18034

Additional Information:

One website gives William's birth as Bellfields, Surrey, with him attesting at Guildford. It also gives two Regiments, the second being Royal Horse Artillery No. 797006. If this is correct William can be found on the 1901 Census living with his parents at Worplesden, near Guildford. His father was a carter in a brickyard. William married Rose in 1913 but no children can be traced.

The Northampton Daily Echo reported "Driver William Tidey of RFA died from gas poisoning during a drill on the use of a new gas helmet. He was one of about 100 men being instructed in the use of anti-gas helmets. When he went into a room where gas was released he was heard to say "Let me out" and pulled at his mask and rushed to the door. Another man also left. He appeared alright but later both men were taken ill. William died but the other man recovered. He was thought not to be wearing his helmet correctly and died of gas poisoning."

Family:

William was one of eleven children, Carry, Edith, Harry, Fred (who died young), Louisa, Percy, Alice, Fred (name re-used), Rose and Harriett.

Francis Edward TRAVELL
(CWGC has name as Travill)

Nationality:	British
Rank:	Private
Service No:	200012
Regiment:	Northamptonshire
Unit:	4th Battalion
Age at Death:	44
Date of Death:	3rd May 1918
Place of Death:	Uckfield Registration District
Parents:	John and Annie Travell
Wife:	Annie Rachel Travell (nee Rockingham)
Address:	34 Abbey Street, Northampton
Grave Ref:	464.I.18014
Medals/Awards:	1915 Star, British and Victory

Additional Information:

The 1881 Census showed Francis living with his parents at 10 Melbourne Road, Duston. His father was a labourer. By the time of the 1911 Census Francis was married to Annie and they lived at 35 Abbey Street, Northampton. He was a shoe finisher.

His medal card showed that he served in the Balkans and was probably wounded there. The 1/4th Battalion embarked from Liverpool in July 1915 and moved to Gallipoli via Mudros. It landed at Suvla Bay on 15th August 1915, and was evacuated to Alexandria on 19th December 1915. It served the rest of the war in Egypt and Palestine.

Francis appears to have joined the 1/4th Territorial Force in about 1908 when it was formed from the previous 1st Volunteer Force and was given the number Private 92. Sometime later, the 1/4th was renumbered and he was given the number 200012. These new numbers started from 200000.

Family:

Francis had four siblings, Agnes, Ernest, Clara and Robert. He had one child, Lily May, born in 1896.

David WALKER
(Served as David Brown)

Nationality:	British
Rank:	Corporal
Service No:	290534
Regiment:	Cameronians (Scottish Rifles)
Unit:	9th Battalion
Age at Death:	23
Date of Death:	22nd February 1918
Place of Death:	Brixworth Registration District
Parents:	Mrs C Walker
Address:	152 Castlebank Street, Partick, Glasgow
Grave Ref:	447.3.17376
Medals/Awards:	1915 Star, British, and Victory

Additional Information:

David's medal card showed that he joined the $1/8^{th}$ Battalion Scottish Rifles (Territorial Force) as Private No. 9974 and went with a draft to reinforce the battalion after it left Gallipoli. The draft left the UK on 2nd December 1915, thus he was awarded the 1915 Star.

He was renumbered as Corporal No. 290534 still with the Scottish Rifles now in Egypt. Later still he appeared to have transferred to the 9th Battalion Scottish Rifles that was serving in France. It is not known whether he actually went to France.

The Northampton Daily Echo, in a report of his funeral, stated that David died at Thornby Auxiliary Military Hospital and that Mrs Mildmay, a nurse, and three patients were among the mourners.

George WELLS

Nationality:	British
Rank:	Private
Service No:	6712
Regiment:	Cheshire
Unit:	Depot
Age at Death:	35
Date of Death:	2nd October 1918
Place of Death:	Northampton
Parents:	Thomas and Mary Ann Wells
Wife:	Florence Wells (nee Snedker)
Address:	30 Leicester Street, Northampton
Grave Ref:	446.4.17333
Medals/Awards:	1914 Star, British, Victory and the Silver War Badge

Additional Information:

The 1881 Census showed George living with his parents in Northampton. His father was a boot maker.

He enlisted into the Cheshire Regiment on 21st November 1901 until 24th November 1904. He stayed on the Reserves. He re-engaged on 21st November 1913 and was mobilized on 5th August 1914. He went to France on 12th September 1914 and returned home on 6th December 1915.

His Service Record showed him being an exchanged Prisoner of War admitted to the Queen Alexandra Military Extension Hospital, Millbank. He was sent home from that hospital on 30th December 1915 to await admission to Roehampton House. This was a specialist hospital for fitting prosthetic limbs.

The Northampton Daily Chronicle reported that George died at Northampton Hospital. He had been a prisoner of war at Wittenburg Camp, Germany for 14 months. George was returned to England as he had lost both feet. He was fitted with artificial ones and discharged. The British Chrome Tanning Co. employed him as a time keeper.

His death was due to internal complications reportedly due to his suffering as a prisoner of war.

Family:

George had nine siblings, Charles, Harry, John Thomas, Wallace, Harriet, Alice, Fred and William.

He married Florence Snedker and they had four children, Doris Winifred; Harriet Kathleen; George who was born and died in 1914; and George born 1917 (name re-used).

Florence's brother James was also buried in the same War Graves Section of Towcester Cemetery having died on 27th October 1918. (see page 187)

Layout of Wittenburg Camp

A lack of basic amenities at this camp, such as fuel for stoves; prisoners having to wash outside in water troughs; and a lack of mattresses in the camp hospital; contributed to a serious typhus epidemic in 1914. An unusual feature of the camp was the bridge over the fence (bottom right of the picture) which served as the main entrance.

Percy William WHITBREAD

Nationality:	British
Rank:	Leading Aircraftman
Service No:	1049679
Regiment:	Royal Air Force Volunteer Reserve
Age at Death:	20
Date of Death:	10th October 1943
Place of Death:	Fylde Registration District
Parents:	Percy John & Helena Maud Whitbread (nee May)
Address:	Far Cotton, Northampton
Grave Ref:	444.17263

Additional Information:

The Northampton Daily Chronicle reported that Percy died at RAF Hospital Kirkham.

The Chronicle also reported that he was the son of Mr Whitbread of Pleydell Road, brother of Helen, Kitty, Hilda and Laura and grandson of Mrs York of Wycliffe Road.

Laura was possibly Percy's twin sister as their births were both registered in the June quarter of 1923 in Northampton.

Albert E WHITE

Nationality:	British
Rank:	Private
Service No:	39516
Regiment:	Bedfordshire
Unit:	4th Battalion
Age at Death:	41
Date of Death:	8th December 1917
Place of Death:	Northampton
Grave Ref:	447.4.1738
Medals/Awards:	Victory and British

Additional Information:

Albert's Medal Card does not give any indication that he served overseas.

The Northampton Daily Chronicle records that the funeral of Private A E White, who died at Northampton Hospital, took place with military honours provided by the Depot. Relatives from Notting Hill attended.

There is a record of an Albert Edward White on the 1911 Census aged 35 and living in Notting Hill. This ties with Albert's age at death and the residence of his relatives. If this is the correct Albert, he had a wife Sarah Elizabeth White, aged 40, and they had been married 8 years with no children. Albert worked as a catering assistant. Also living with them was an Emily Amelia Jewell his sister-in-law.

Joseph WILKINSON

Nationality:	British
Rank:	Driver
Service No:	T/39336
Regiment:	Royal Army Service Corps (RASC)
Unit:	1st Cavalry Division Horse Transport Company
Formerly:	3rd Battalion Northants Regiment
Age at Death:	34
Date of Death:	3rd April 1920
Place of Death:	Ministry of Pensions Hospital, Victoria Park, Leicester
Parents:	Anthony and Elizabeth Wilkinson
Wife:	Gertrude L Wilkinson (nee Travell)
Address:	26 Silver Street, Northampton
Grave Ref:	445.4.17301
Medals/Awards:	1914 Star, Victory and British

Additional Information:

The 1901 Census showed Joseph living with his parents and working as a general labourer. They were living at Adnitt Place, Northampton.

Joseph's Medal Record showed that he went to France on 20th September 1914 with a draft for the 1st Battalion Northamptonshire Regiment with the service No. 3/10349. He must have later transferred to the RASC.

Family:

Joseph apparently had five siblings, Elizabeth, George, Alice, John and Clare.

Fred WILLS

Nationality:	British
Rank:	Private
Service No:	22198
Regiment:	Suffolk
Unit:	12th Battalion
Age at Death:	17
Date of Death:	2nd November 1915
Place of Death:	Farnham Registration District
Parents:	Frederick and Annie Wills
Address:	48 Junction Road, Kingsley Road, Northampton
Grave Ref:	448.2.17415

Additional Information:

The 1911 Census showed Fred living with his parents at 87 Somerset Street, Northampton and at school but working as a newsboy.

No service or medal record could be found.

The Northampton Daily Echo reported that "the funeral took place on 6th November with full military honours of Private Fred Wills, D Company 12th Battalion Suffolk Regiment who died in Frensham Hospital, Farnham on Thursday from erysipelas and pleurisy. The body was brought from Aldershot to Northampton on Friday. Fred joined the army about two years ago. He was the son of Mr and Mrs F Wills at 74 Junction Road. A firing party and escort were provided by the Depot. The funeral was held at St Matthews Church before going on to Towcester Road. Mourners included his brothers, Mr Walter Wills and Corporal Charles Wills, who was also serving in the 12th Battalion Suffolk Regiment."

Family:

Fred had five, possibly six siblings, William, Charles, Maud, Kate and Walter. There was also a George on the 1901 Census.

Thomas WILLS

Nationality: British
Rank: Private
Service No: 1185
Regiment: Northamptonshire Yeomanry
Transferred to: Labour Corps
Age at Death: 27
Date of Death: 13th November 1918
Place of Death: Northampton
Grave Ref: 446.4.17317
Medals/Awards: British and Victory

Additional Information:

Thomas appears to have had three service numbers. The one shown above; a second with the Northamptonshire Yeomanry, Private No. 145425; and the third with the Labour Corps, No. 504636. All these were shown on his medal card.

Apart from Thomas's medal card we have been unable to verify any other information.

Cap Badge of the Northamptonshire Yeomanry

Walter John Thomas WOOD

Nationality:	British
Rank:	Private
Service No:	9646
Regiment:	Northamptonshire
Unit:	1st Battalion
Age at Death:	25
Date of Death:	4th March 1919
Place of Death:	Northampton
Parents:	Walter Thomas and Sarah Ann Wood (nee Knibbs)
Wife:	Amy P Wood (nee Bosworth)
Address:	77 Ethel Street, Northampton
Grave Ref:	445.2.17303
Medals/Awards:	1914 Star, Victory and British

Additional Information:

The 1911 Census showed Walter living with his parents at the Duke of York, Oxford Street, Wellingborough where his father was the publican. Walter was educated at Wellingborough Grammar School.

Walter would have joined the Regiment in about 1913 at the Depot. Later he was posted to the 1st Battalion based at Blackdown, Aldershot.

From Blackdown he went to France on 13th August 1914 and could have been at Mons, Marne and Ypres. According to one report Walter was captured on 27th August, 1914 with a broken leg. After his capture he spent time as a prisoner of war at Sennelager and was brutalised, according to one report, because he was a German speaker. He was moved to Berlin, found guilty of insubordination and inciting to mutiny, and was sentenced to three months hard labour.

In early 1917 he was transferred to Switzerland and was living at Hotel Edelweiss, Murren. An appeal was made by the Independent Newspaper for the public to adopt a prisoner of war. The women and manageress, Miss Amy Bosworth, working at Church & Roberts, blouse makers of St Edmunds Road, responded and sent parcels to Walter who wrote back thanking them.

When repatriated from Switzerland he visited Amy Bosworth and the women to thank them personally. He became romantically involved with Amy and they married at the Unitarian Church, on 18th December 1918. Three months later he fell ill and died of double pneumonia at Duston Hospital.

Walter and Amy's marriage in December 1918

Family:

Walter (known as Jack) had seven siblings, Elizabeth, Arthur, Edith, Ben (known as Ted), Kathleen, Harold and Fred.

The family, except for Walter, left for Australia sometime after the 1911 Census. His mother Sarah and six of the children are found on the shipping list for the Miltiades which left London on 26th April 1913.

Walter's brother, Arthur, made two attempts to enlist and finally enlisted having lied about his age. He was allocated to the 18th Battalion of the Australian Infantry (Private No. 2217) and arrived at Étaples on 4th April 1916. He was killed on 1st May 1916 having been moved into the line on 23rd April 1916. Arthur was buried at Brewery Orchard Cemetery, Bois-Grenier.

On the CWGC site, Arthur's parents are listed as living at Cambridge Park, Kingswood, New South Wales, Australia.

The Wood family in Australia

The Rushden and District Historical Society have a more in-depth history of this family which can be found at www.rushdenheritage.co.uk

David Charles WYATT

Nationality:	British
Rank:	Lance Corporal
Service No:	71063
Regiment:	Royal Engineers
Unit:	43rd Air Line Section
Age at Death:	45
Date of Death:	2nd July 1917
Place of Death:	Thetford Registration District
Parents:	William and Isabella Wyatt
Wife:	Emily Wyatt (nee Mills)
Address:	46 Essex Street, Northampton
Grave Ref:	448.4.17385
Medals/Awards:	Victory and British

Additional Information:

The 1891 Census showed David serving as a Private No. 2971 with the 1st Battalion, Northamptonshire Regiment based at the Aldershot

Barracks. He went with the Battalion to India in 1892. The photograph above was taken while David was in India.

The 1911 Census showed David living with his family and working as a wireman for a telephone company. It was this experience which found him in the Royal Engineers Cable and Air Line Section which was a signalling unit.

The Northampton Daily Echo reported that "Lance Corporal David C Wyatt, Royal Engineers whose wife lives at 46 Essex Street, died at Camp Hospital, Thetford from haemorrhage to the brain. He served in France for 12 months and was wounded on 7th February 1917 and invalided back to England. He had served for 16 years in the Northamptonshire Regiment going to India and the Boer War. The funeral service was held at the Roman Catholic Cathedral and the Training Battalion provided the escort and bearers to Towcester Road."

For his service prior to the First World War David was awarded the India General Service Medal with clasps for Punjab Frontier, Samana and Tira, plus the Queen's South Africa Medal with clasps for Belmont, Modder River, Transvaal and Orange Free State and the King's South Africa Medal with clasps for 1901 and 1902.

Family:

David had 5 siblings, William, Catherine, Winifred, David and Amelia.

He and Emily had 9 children, Kate, Herbert, Phyliss, Winifred, David, Doris, Frank, Leonard and Gladys.

William George YORK

Nationality:	British
Rank:	Private
Service No:	9123
Regiment:	Worcestershire
Unit:	2nd Battalion
Age at Death:	30 (Death Registration says 29)
Date of Death:	9th September 1916
Place of Death:	Northampton
Parents:	William John and Louisa York
Address:	13 Augustine Street, Northampton
Grave Ref:	448.3.17400
Medals/Awards:	Victory and British

Additional Information:

The 1891 Census showed William living with his parents in Northampton. His father was a brewer's labourer. William does not appear on the 1901 or 1911 Census.

William attested on 22nd February 1905 at Sandown, Isle of Wight with the Worcestershire Regiment. He mentioned that he had been in the Militia and was aged 18 years and 11 months born in Wollaston. He was posted to Templemore in Ireland. In November 1905 he was posted to Malta and stayed there until May 1906. William then spent a short time in Egypt before returning to Malta in June 1906 and was there until leaving for India in November 1908. He was based at Bareilly in Uttar Pradesh with B Company 4th Battalion Worcester Regiment until December 1912. He returned to the UK and was put on the Army Reserve.

When he was recalled to the Worcestershire Regiment he had been working for the Northampton Brewery Co and went to France with the 2nd Battalion on 14th August 1914. He was wounded by shrapnel in both arms and ankle at Ypres on 6th November 1914 and sent to Rouen Hospital. On 15th December he was returned to England on SS St David.

He remained in England but on 9th September 1916 he was sent to the Duston War Hospital with a problem with a wound to the right lung. He was diagnosed with empyema with abscess on his lungs and died the same day.

Family:

William had two younger brothers, Frank and Alfred who were still living with their parents at 13 St Augustine Street, Northampton at the time of the 1911 Census.

Ambulance train used to bring wounded to hospitals in the UK

CZECHOSLOVAKIAN BURIALS

Following the Anschluss (Union) of Nazi Germany and Austria in 1938, the conquest of Czechoslovakia became Hitler's next ambition. Despite appeasement attempts by Neville Chamberlain with the Munich Pact of September 1938, the German Army marched into the Sudeten parts of Bohemia and Moravia in March 1939. A Czech government-in-exile installed itself in London and many Czechs, who were of Jewish origins or otherwise anti-Nazi, departed to Russia and Poland, some thence to France.

A Franco-Czech treaty of October 1939 allowed for the reconstruction of the Czech Army on French territory. The Czechs were to be incorporated into the French Foreign Legion, but after France's entry into WW2, the 1st Czech Infantry Division was created, on 24th January 1940.

During the Battle of France its two regiments fought rear-guard actions against the German 16th Panzer Division. They eventually withdrew to the southern town of Narbonne and were evacuated to Britain from the port of Sete.

The first Czech army camp was established at Cholmondeley Castle near Chester. The various units were re-grouped into motorized infantry and moved to new bases. In September 1943 the HQ of a new Czech Independent Armoured Brigade was established at The Manor, Arthingworth. Units of the Brigade were quartered all over east Northants, including Brixworth, Lamport, Loddington, Finedon and Deene.

The Brigade left Northants in May 1944 in preparation for the D-Day landings. It was eventually responsible for attacking and besieging the German garrison in Dunkirk, in October 1944. After it accepted the German surrender there, the Brigade pushed on into Germany and eventually regained the troops' homeland on 1st May 1945. On that day the Czech Independent Armoured Brigade joyously crossed the border, back to Czechoslovakia.

However, the Brigade left six soldiers in Northamptonshire. They died from causes mostly unknown, between November 1943 and June 1944 and lie in graves in two locations. Their graves are maintained by the Commonwealth War Graves Commission. The CWGC maintains all Czechoslovakian War Graves in the United Kingdom as part of a reciprocal arrangement and the Czech and Slovakian Governments maintain British War Graves in their countries.

Three are buried in Kingsthorpe Cemetery and three in the Jewish section of Towcester Road. The men buried in Towcester Road are:

Jiříl EHRMANN, born 16th September 1903, Spálené Poříči, okres Pizeň (now in the Czech Republic) – served as a vojín (private) in the 1st Czech Tank Brigade, service no. R2288). He died on 13th May 1944 in Arthingworth. The notes use the word 'sebevražda' which translates as 'suicide'.

Leopold GERSTMANN, born 21st September 1907, Brno (now in the Czech Republic) – served as a vojín in the Czech Independent Armoured Brigade, service no. R1817. He died on 23rd March 1944 in Kettering General Hospital.

Bedřich Karel STEIN, born 5th January 1915 in Saarbrücken, Německo, (Germany) and served as a vojín in the 1st Czech Tank Brigade, service no. R2221. He died on 11th May 1944 (CWGC states 7th May) in Northampton.

Gerstmann   Stein   Ehrmann

GERMAN BURIALS

The centennial of the Great War is to be a period of international remembrance, and of reconciliation. In this spirit we also commemorate the ten German nationals who were originally buried in graves at Towcester Road.

All but one of these were soldiers in the Imperial German Army, who arrived in Northamptonshire as Prisoners of War [PoW]. The exception was an Internee, Karl Wiedemann, probably a merchant seaman, who would have been detained early in the war at the Pattishall (Eastcote) Camp, near Northampton. He died at Northampton General Hospital on 13th May 1915 and was buried at Towcester Road.

Pattishall Camp had been established specifically for Internees, under the auspices of the National Sailors' and Firemen's Union [NSFU]. Before the war many German nationals served as seamen on British merchant ships. At the outbreak of hostilities, they were interned, along with other civilians of German nationality. The NSFU petitioned to control the camp at Pattishall, to ensure a reasonable standard of captivity for their seafaring colleagues. Pattishall was handed over to the military authorities in October 1915, to become a camp for the growing numbers of combatant PoWs.

Courtesy of C R Chapman

Pattishall Camp C1916

The military men all died between the 7th November 1918 and 9th January 1919, at the Upton War Hospital, Duston. Some may have been PoWs at Pattishall, or transferred from other parts of the county, such as Oundle or Rothwell. They succumbed to the influenza pandemic which afflicted a large part of the world at this time, and which accounted for even more deaths than the war itself.

On the 16th October 1959 an agreement was concluded between the United Kingdom and Federal German governments to establish a central German Military Cemetery at Cannock Chase in Staffordshire. The bodies of most of the German war dead buried in Great Britain and Northern Ireland from both world wars were transferred there. They were mostly PoWs, but also airship and aircraft crews, and sailors whose bodies were washed ashore.

The ten war graves of Towcester Road were transferred to Cannock Chase in the early 1960s, and the Cemetery was finally opened to the public on 10th June 1967. The burials are in a distinct row of five graves, marked by headstones of grey Belgian granite. Each stone bears two names, with ranks and dates of death, as shown in the accompanying photograph.

The Cemetery is maintained by the Commonwealth War Graves Commission on behalf of the German War Graves Commission. In addition to Cannock Chase, another 147 graves containing 263 German dead of the Great War are buried in cemeteries elsewhere in Britain, also maintained by the CWGC.

Jean BAILLEUL – Gefreiter (Lance Corporal) died 9th November 1918, aged 28

Franz BÜSER – Kanonier (Gunner), in the 12th Infantry, died 21st December 1918, aged 26

Albert O KRÖNER - Soldat (Soldier), PoW No. 29948 in the 181th Infantry, died 7th January 1919, aged 34

Freidrich LINDER - Soldat (Soldier), PoW No. 23252 in the 104th Infantry, died 9th January 1919, aged 20

Theodor NORDHAUS, - Infanterist (Infantryman) in the 71st Infantry, died 16th November 1918, aged 28

Max REISE – Soldat (Soldier) in the 453rd Infantry, died 14th November 1918, aged 21

Theodor SCHEIDERICH – Gefreiter (Lance Corporal) in the 237th Infantry, died 17th November 1918, aged 20

Max STÄCKER (death registration is in the name STÖCKER) - PoW No. 22877, Schutze (Marksman), died 7th November 1918, aged 21

Franz STRICKFADEN (death registration is in the name Streckfarden) - Soldat (Soldier) in the 470th Infantry, died 23rd November 1918, aged 21

Karl WIEDEMANN (Carl Wiedermann) - Internierter (Internee) died 13th May 1915, aged 45

Photograph Copyright Geoff Grainger 2013
Five Graves of the Men Listed Above
German Military Cemetery, Cannock Chase

Many Regiments passed through Northampton during the course of the First World War.

Courtesy of Doug Goddard

The Cheshire Regiment in Guildhall Road

The Welsh Regiment making friends with the locals

CAMPAIGN MEDALS AND AWARDS

WORLD WAR ONE

The 1914 Star or 1914-15 Star together with the Victory and British medals are known as Pip, Squeak and Wilfred but if only the British and Victory were awarded they are known as Mutt and Jeff

The 1914 Star

Issued to people who served in France or Belgium between 5th August 1914 to midnight on 22nd November 1914 inclusive. The award was open to officers and men of the British Expeditionary Forces, doctors and nurses as well as Royal Navy, Royal Marines, Royal Naval Reserve and Royal Naval Volunteer Reserve who served ashore with the Royal Naval Division in France or Belgium.

A narrow horizontal bronze clasp sewn onto the ribbon, bearing the dates 5th AUG - 22nd NOV 1914 shows that the recipient had actually served under fire of the enemy during that period. Recipients who received the medal with the clasp were also entitled to attach a small silver heraldic rose to the ribbon when just the ribbon was being worn.

The 1914-15 Star

This bronze medal is very similar to the 1914 Star but it was issued to a much wider range of recipients. It was awarded to all who served in any theatre of war against Germany between 5th August 1914 and 31st December 1915, except those eligible for the 1914 Star. Similarly those who received the Africa General Service Medal or the Sudan 1910 Medal were not eligible for the award. To receive this medal the recipients had to have been awarded the British and Victory Medals.

The British War Medal, 1914-18

The silver or bronze medal was awarded to officers and men of the British and Imperial Forces who either entered a theatre of war or entered service overseas between 5th August 1914 and 11th November

1918 inclusive. This was later extended to services in Russia, Siberia and some other areas in 1919 and 1920.

The Allied Victory Medal

Eligibility for this medal was more restrictive and not everyone who received the British War Medal also received the Victory Medal.

The Territorial Force War Medal 1914-1919

Only members of the Territorial Force and Territorial Force Nursing Service were eligible for this medal. They had to have been a member of the Territorial Force on or before 30th September 1914 and to have served in an operational theatre of war outside the United Kingdom between 5th August 1914 and 11th November 1918. An individual who was eligible to receive the 1914 Star or 1914/15 Star could not receive the Territorial War Medal.

The Silver War Badge

The badge was originally issued to officers and men who were discharged or retired from the military forces as a result of sickness or injury caused by their war service. After April 1918 the eligibility was amended to include civilians serving with the Royal Army Medical Corps, female nurses, staff and aid workers. It became known as the "Services Rendered Badge". The recipient would also receive a certificate with the badge.

Mercantile Marine War Medal

The Board of Trade awarded this campaign medal to men who had served in the Merchant Navy and who had made a voyage through a war zone or danger zone during the 1914-18 war.

Next of Kin Memorial Plaque and Scroll

From 1919, and for several years after the end of the Great War, over a million plaques and scrolls were sent to next of kin in commemoration of their soldiers, sailors, airmen and a few hundred women, who died as a direct consequence of service. All those who died between 4th August 1914 and 30th April 1919 whilst in military service in the battlegrounds of the theatres of war and in the Dominions, as a result of sickness, suicide or accidents in the Home Establishments (within the United Kingdom), or as a result of wounds incurred during their time in military service were commemorated on a plaque and a scroll.

The next of kin of the 306 British and Commonwealth military personnel who were executed following a Court Martial did not receive a memorial plaque.

Approximately 600 memorial plaques were issued to the next of kin of women who died as a direct consequence of their involvement in the Great War.

Where Australians Rest

This was a booklet distributed to the next of kin of each soldier who died with the Australian Imperial Force. It is 73 pages long and has details plus pen drawings of the war cemeteries in all the First World War theatres of war plus two in England, Harefield and Brookwood. It was distributed to the next of kin of all the soldiers who died during the war.

Anzac Commemorative Medallion and Badge

This medallion was instituted in 1967. It was awarded to surviving members of the Australian forces who served on the Gallipoli Peninsula, or in direct support of the operations from close off shore, at any time during the period from the first Anzac Day in April 1915 to the date of the final evacuation in January 1916. Next of kin, or other entitled persons, were entitled to receive the medallion on behalf of their relatives.

South African War Medals received by some of the regular soldiers prior to the First World War

Queen's Sudan Medal commemorates the forced expansion of the de facto British protectorate of Egypt to the south, into what at the time was a wholly independent Sudan. The campaign began on 7th June 1896 mainly with Egyptian troops, but later reinforced with two British brigades, one of which was present at "The Atbara", and then both at Omdurman.

Khedive's Sudan Medal was instituted on 12th February 1897 on the approval of Abbas Hilmi Pasha, Khedive of Egypt, initially to commemorate the re-conquest of the Dongola province and later included battles up to 1908.

Queen's South Africa Medal was awarded for campaigns between 1899-1902. The Relief of Ladysmith clasp was awarded to all troops in Natal, north of and including Estcourt between 15th December 1899 and 28th February 1900. The Tugela Heights clasp was awarded to troops employed in operations north of an east and west line through Chieveley Station between 14th and 17th February, 1900. The Laing's Nek clasp was awarded to all troops employed in the operations north of an east and west line through Newcastle between 2nd and 9th June 1900. The Transvaal clasp awarded to all troops in the Transvaal between 24th May 1900 and 31st May 1902.

King's South Africa Medal 1901-1902 – This second campaign medal for the South African or 'Boer War' was instituted in 1902 and awarded to all who were in theatre on or after the 1st January 1902, and had completed 18 months' service prior to 1st June 1901. The medal was to recognise service in the difficult latter phases of the war. It was never awarded singly and was paired with the Queen's South Africa Medal.

SITE PLAN

Fourth Row	97 – 112		113 - 130	
Third Row	65 - 80	Memorial	81 - 92	93 - 96
Second Row	33 - 48	Cross	45 - 60	61 - 64
Front Row	1 - 16		17 - 28	29 - 32

Grave No.	Surname	First Names
23	Abbot	John (Jack)
71	Adams	Benjamin
118	Alexander	James William
29	Amos	John Thomas
111	Ashby	Albert
97	Ashton	George
95	Ayres	John Joseph
92	Barker	Edward
128	Barnes	George Albert
94	Batchelor	Reginald Victor
122	Bavington	Harry Arthur Esau
85	Bazeley	George Quest
103	Booke	James
62	Bull	Joseph Cyril
33	Bunton	Edward George
6	Burnett	Harold James
102	Cadd	Cecil Leonard
38	Calder	William
21	Campbell	William Argyle
35	Carroll	Thomas
124	Carter	Harry N
63	Chambers	Arthur Alfred
36	Chambers	Percy
59	Chandler	Robert James
108	Chapman	George
24	Clark	Albert Lewis
32	Clements	Alice Annie
43	Codling	Arthur
73	Collier	William Harold

Grave No.	Surname	First Names
98	Collishaw	William
79	Comber	Sidney John
19	Comley	William Tait
115	Cooke	Samuel Robert
99	Cope	Ernest Edward
64	Cosford	Arthur Edward
51	Cowell	Thomas George
121	Cox	Frederick
22	Cox	Lyle Hampden
1	Cox	Walter Charles Ebden
39	Curtis	Clarence William
87	Dawson	Percy Mordecai
14	Day	Walter James
25	Deacon	Frederick George
77	Denton	Harry
129	Dixon	Rollo Edward
4	Doust	Roy
46	Dove	Harry Percy
107	Durley	Charles Lewis
34	Durrant	James Henry
20	Eales	Charles
84	Easton	George Campbell
96	Eldred	Harold (Harry)
112	Eley	William Emanuel
8	Elliott	Arthur Pearson
74	Falla	William
86	Fitzhugh	Alfred
55	Frost	Harry
68	Gardner	Walter Thomas
114	Garner	James Fleming
31	Garrett	Glendon Kenneth
125	Gascoigne	William Thomas
7	Goacher	William Edward
109	Goodsall	William
126	Gorzkiewicz	Marian
110	Hamer	Nathan
50	Hancock	George William
58	Hayes	Denis

Grave No.	Surname	First Names
106	Hickman	William
127	Holloway	Ronald
9	Hollway	James Clinton
18	Holmes	William James
47	Inns	Phillip Robert Hector
41	Jenner	Henry
69	Johnson	Thomas
13	Jones	Arthur
12	Jones	Harry
17	Kelly	William Joseph
42	Kendall	Charles Robert
116	Kennedy	Herbert Victor
91	Land	Francis William
10	Lapworth	Frederick Thomas Debron
101	Latham	Peter Walter
81	Lee	Edwin James
54	Lewis	Thomas
16	Lucas	William Edward
60	Luck	Thomas
40	Maxwell	John Arthur
75	McCann	William
104	McGoldrick	Charles Henry
113	Mein	Ernest
26	Mills	Edward
67	Moore	Charles
89	Musgrove	Frederick
27	Nash	Frederick
11	Newton	David
66	O'Grady	Joseph
90	Percival	John Litchfield
48	Pittam	Christopher George
56	Pittams	Arthur Ernest
82	Reeve	George
76	Riddle	Joseph
119	Robinson	Arthur
105	Robinson	George
13	Ross	William

Grave No.	Surname	First Names
80	Scanes	Reginald Clarence
3	Seal	Arthur Thomas
52	Sims	John
2	Slater	Benjamin
28	Smith	James
61	Smith	Kenneth George
37	Smith	Levi
123	Smith	Walter
83	Snedker	James
88	Southworth	John
117	Stocker	Percy
30	Summerford	Leslie Charles
65	Swann	Alfred Robert
70	Taggart	John William
5	Tidy	William
15	Travell	Francis Edward
78	Walker	David
49	Wells	George
130	Whitbread	Percy William
45	White	Albert E
57	Wilkinson	Joseph
100	Wills	Fred
53	Wills	Thomas
120	Wood	Walter John Thomas
44	Wyatt	David Charles
72	York	William George

Men not buried in the war graves section

Grave No.	Surname	First Names
10648	Brown	Herbert Charles
13457	Buxton	George
11588	Hillyer	Harry
5338	Marriott	William
11868	Merriman	William
6278	Sephton	Glynn
12512	Smith	Ellis Victor Ashby
7294	Tibbs	Albert Edward

SOURCES

The sources used were the same for all the biographies and are listed below. Where information outside these sources was used it is shown at the bottom of the individual biography.

Ancestry.co.uk – Family Trees and other documentation
Australian National Archives – full service records available free on-line
Australian War Memorial
Birth, Marriage and Death Index – FreeBMD – England and Wales
Canada, Library and Archives – first and last page of service record
Census UK – 1881, 1891, 1901 and 1911
Commonwealth War Grave Commission
Electoral Rolls
Familysearch.org
Find my Past
Forces War Records
Kelly's Directories
London Gazette
Medal Record Cards
Military Tribunal Records
Northampton Daily Echo
Northampton Chronicle
Northampton Mercury
Northampton Borough Cemetery Office
Northampton Record Office
Northamptonshire and the Great War 1914-1918, by W H Holloway 1920
Northants Family Tree Net
Pension Records
Regimental War Diaries
Scotland's People
Service Records
Silver War Badge Records
The Independent (Northampton)
UK Army Roll of Honour

Alison Butler has carried out a detailed study of the Australians buried at Towcester Road Cemetery, and other cemeteries in Northamptonshire. It will be published in 2015 titled, Northampton ANZACS.

Towcester Road Cemetery
Northampton
NN4 8LS